9/30/81

Good wishes
to
J. David DeLozier—

Sincerely,

Art Lerner

D0773027

Poetry
in the
Therapeutic Experience

POETRY
IN THE
THERAPEUTIC EXPERIENCE

Edited by
Arthur Lerner, Ph.D.

Pergamon Press

NEW YORK • TORONTO • OXFORD • SYDNEY • FRANKFURT • PARIS

Pergamon Press Offices:

U.S.A.	Pergamon Press Inc., Maxwell House, Fairview Park, Elmsford, New York 10523, U.S.A.
U.K.	Pergamon Press Ltd., Headington Hill Hall, Oxford OX3, OBW, England
CANADA	Pergamon of Canada, Ltd., 75 The East Mall, Toronto, Ontario M8Z 5W3 Canada
AUSTRALIA	Pergamon Press (Aust) Pty. Ltd., 19a Boundary Street, Rushcutters Bay, N.S.W. 2011, Australia
FRANCE	Pergamon Press SARL, 24 Rue des Ecoles, 75240 Paris, Cedex 05, France
WEST GERMANY	Pergamon Press GmbH, 6242 Kronberg/Taunus, Pferdstrasse 1, West Germany

Copyright © 1978 Pergamon Press Inc.

Library of Congress Cataloging in Publication Data

Main entry under title:

Poetry in the therapeutic experience.

Includes index.
1. Poetry - - Therapeutic use. I. Lerner,
Arthur. [DNLM: 1. Poetry. 1. Bibliotherapy.
WM450 P745]
RC489.P6P63   616.8'916'6   77-24999
ISBN 0-08-022222-6

All Rights Reserved. No part of this publication may be reproduced, stored in a retrieval system or transmitted in any form or by any means: electronic, electrostatic, magnetic tape, mechanical, photocopying, recording or otherwise, without permission in writing from the publishers.

PRINTED IN THE UNITED STATES OF AMERICA

to
MATILDA

Contents

CONTRIBUTORS

Allan S. Abrams, M.D.
Private Practice, Child, Adolescent and
General Psychiatry, Woodland Hills, California;
Assistant Clinical Professor of Psychiatry
School of Medicine, University of Southern California,
Los Angeles, California

Charles Ansell, Ed.D.
Senior Training Analyst
Los Angeles Society for Psychoanalytic Psychology;
Member, Board of Directors
California School of Professional Psychology;
Member, Advisory Board
Poetry Therapy Institute;
Private Practice, Encino, California

Franklin M. Berry, Ph.D.
Associate Professor of Psychology
Columbus College
Columbus, Georgia;
Experimental Psychologist

Mary Clancy, M.S.
Senior Rehabilitation Counselor
California Department of Rehabilitation
San Francisco, California

Louise Davis, M.A.
Supervising Facilitator
Poetry Therapy Institute
Encino, California;
Poetry Therapy Facilitator
Woodview-Calabasas Hospital
Calabasas, California

Ken Edgar, Ph.D.
Professor of Psychology
Indiana University of Pennsylvania
Indiana, Pennsylvania
Clinical Psychologist and Novelist

Julius Griffin, M.D.
Founder and Medical Director
Griffin Psychiatric Clinic
Encino, California;
Board of Directors
Poetry Therapy Institute
Encino, California

Dominick E. Grundy, Ph.D.
Assistant Professor of English
Nassau Community College
Garden City, Long Island, N.Y.;
Staff Counselor
Institute for Sociotherapy
New York, N.Y.

Owen E. Heninger, M.D.
Director, Continuing Medical Education
Poetry Therapy Institute
Encino, California;
Psychiatrist, Private Practice,
Whittier, California

Roger Lauer, M.D.
Lecturer, Department of Psychiatry
School of Medicine
University of California, San Francisco;
Private Practice, San Francisco, California

Arthur Lerner, Ph.D.
Professor of Psychology
Los Angeles City College
Los Angeles, California;
Founder and Director
Poetry Therapy Institute
Encino, California;
Director of Poetry Therapy
Woodview-Calabasas Hospital
Calabasas, California

Robert N. Ross, Ph.D.
National Institute of Mental Health
Research Fellow
Boston University School of Medicine
Division of Psychiatry
Boston, Massachusetts

Gilbert A. Schloss, Ph.D.
Assistant Professor of Psychology
Manhattan College
Bronx, New York;
Director, Creative Arts Therapies
Institute for Sociotherapy
New York, N.Y.

Edward Stainbrook, Ph.D., M.D.
Professor and Chairman
Department of Human Behavior
School of Medicine
University of Southern California
Los Angeles, California

Preface

The ancient Greeks have told us that Asclepius, the god of healing, was the son of Apollo, god of reason and poetry. Here are some thoughts from poets and healers of our own time that imply a similar kinship:

> Poetry is the response of our innermost being to the ecstasy, the agony, and the all-embracing mystery of life. It is a song, or a sigh, or a cry, often all of them together. Thus, we are really all poets. A few can articulate responses better than others. At best these few speak for the rest of us, and when they do they constitute the noblest of all priesthoods.
>
> Charles Angoff

> Psychotherapy is a process of self-reeducation based on understanding and choice. The therapist facilitates objective distancing, encourages subjective involvement and becomes a significant other person in the client's therapy work. Thus the goal of psychotherapy is to improve and/or maximize the capacity to grow and function within a social context in keeping with the client's needs and wishes.
>
> Michael Shiryon

> Therapy is any procedure which is designed to allow the natural healing tendencies of the organism to restore effective functioning. It is therefore not healing in itself but only a facilitating process toward healing. In psychotherapy, as a special area of therapy, this obviously means working toward producing improvement in self-esteem, interrelationships between the individual and other people and consonance with the cosmos around him. The more flexible and broadly effective the therapeutic procedure, the more applicable it will be to the needs and healing efforts of the individual.
>
> C. H. Hardin Branch

Poetry humanizes because it links the individual by its distilled experience, its rhythms, its words to another in a way which no other form of communication can. Poetry also helps to ease the aloneness which we all share in common.

Myra Cohn Livingston

Psychotherapy is an act of creation; consequently, it is a God-like event. In terms of activity it is the effort of an individual to lift himself from one plane of existence, which causes him discomfort and which does not utilize his potentials, to a higher plane of serenity and efficiency. This can be accomplished alone or with the help of others.

Raymond J. Corsini

Poetry is the language of analogies. Poets place the things they find in this world into arrangements which have sequence and connections. The connections are associational as well as causal. It is the psyche which constructs the patterns that come forth in finished form in the structure of the poem. The relationships seen among objects by poets often echo those that lie immanent in almost everyone.

Ann Stanford

Under the direction of the competent professional, poetry therapy offers a viable modality for reducing the anxiety and hostility that come from a stress-filled world. Used as a form of psychotherapy and self-analysis, poetry therapy provides a means of releasing emotions so as to give the individual a sense of order and purposefulness.

Hirsch Lazaar Silverman

In light of the above, the editor suggests that poetry, like all art forms used in psychotherapy, will make possible the spontaneous union of artistic and scientific experience via the phenomenon of creativity.

Acknowledgments

Poetry in the Therapeutic Experience is the result of myriad efforts representing people from diverse disciplines who have contributed directly or indirectly to its making.

In acknowledging individuals who have helped in the reading and refinement of the manuscript, the editor begins with those who have made major contributions.

Thomas J. McCarthy, Professor of English at Los Angeles City College, read the manuscript in the original and was instrumental in all phases of editing and revision up to and including the final draft.

John Nomland, Periodicals Librarian at Los Angeles City College, made many useful suggestions by clarifying and checking bibliographical and reference materials.

Harold Borko, Professor of Library Science at UCLA, was especially helpful in reading the manuscript and offering suggestions.

Henderson G. Burns, Professor of Psychology at Los Angeles City College, offered cogent comments on some major aspects of psychological theory and their relationship to poetry.

Sylvia M. Halpern, Chief Manuscript Editor at Pergamon Press, was always available with practical suggestions and encouragement.

Matilda Lerner, my wife, to whom this book is dedicated, spent countless hours typing and retyping manuscripts.

* * *

Among others who have contributed to the making of *Poetry in the Therapeutic Experience* are the following:

Los Angeles City College—Marian Cushman, Reference Librarian; Louise Ludwig, Professor of Psychology; Max Sheanin, Chairman, Psychology Department.

xiv

St. Elizabeth's Hospital, Washington, D.C.—Arleen Hynes, Reference Librarian and Bibliotherapist; Ken Gorelick, Psychiatrist.

UCLA Extension—Yolande C. Chambers, Director, Department of Human Development and Services; Mary Earl, Continuing Education Specialist; James S. Hartzell, Coordinator, English Class Programs.

University of Denver—Paul Hunsinger, Professor, Speech Communication.

Los Angeles City Public Library—James F. Saunders, Librarian, Literature Department.

Poetry Therapy Institute, Encino, California:

Board of Directors—Julius Griffin, Psychiatrist; Owen E. Heninger, Psychiatrist; Seymour L. Myers, General Medicine; Anne Ross Silver, Executive Secretary; Keith Van Vliet, Photographer.

Advisory Board Members—Psychologists Ibrahim Abou-Ghorra, Charles Ansell, Gilbert A. Schloss, Everett L. Shostrom, and Edwin S. Shneidman.

Special thanks are extended for original quotes to the following Poetry Therapy Advisory Board Members: Poets Charles Angoff, Myra Cohn Livingston, Ann Stanford; Psychologists Raymond J. Corsini, Michael Shiryon, Hirsch Lazaar Silverman; Psychiatrist C. Hardin Branch, and also to Professors and Poets John Frederick Nims and Molly Harrower; Ted Simmons, Coordinator, Poetry Workshops; and Dr. Leo and Frances Sandron, Coordinators, Psycho-drama Workshops.

Thanks are also due to Rosalyn Griffin, Dr. Charlotte Myers, and Patricia Smith.

Woodview-Calabasas Hospital, Calabasas, California:

Psychiatrists—Allan S. Abrams, William Baumzweiger-Bauer, Vincent Cipriotti, Thomas A. Curtis, William D. Jacoby, Ernest Masler, Joel A. Moskowitz, Donald J. Perry, Alan Satou, Irwin M. Shultz, Mack E. Sturgis, and William R. Flynn, Medical Director.

Psychologists—Sanford Brotman, David Kalman, Mildred G. Mayne, and Bruce Sutkus.

Also, thanks are due Thomas I. Hayes, Jr., Administrator; Paula Morrison, Director, Community Relations; Margaret Davis, Director of Nursing; Barbara Baer, Social Worker; and Staff.

Introduction

Poetry in the Therapeutic Experience assumes that the field known as "poetry therapy" is presently composed of a wide variety of experiences and interests groping for a central theory or rationale. In keeping with this assumption it is the editor's view that as of now the use of poetry in therapy is a tool and not a school. It is also the editor's view that the various schools of psychology can find a place for poetry and other literary genres in their respective frames of reference.

Beyond doubt, poetry therapy is currently in a state of flux. At first glance, one might even say it is in a state of confusion. There are as many different "theories" as there are practitioners in the field. There are even some who believe there is no such phenomenon as poetry therapy. Others believe that poetry therapy is part of bibliotherapy.

Be that as it may, the beginning of any field finds innovators committed to expanding conscious awareness of their particular approach. Recent history suggests, too, that ethics, standards, professional policing, legislation, and certification all become part of any discipline's drive toward professional acceptance.

Poetry in the Therapeutic Experience does not, then, lay claim to final answers. It is rather that the contributors are sharing their special expertise and interests as a means of adding to our information and understanding of the field.

The opening chapter by Dr. Edward Stainbrook considers poetry as part of a psychotherapeutic experience which does not negate mind at the expense of feeling or vice versa. At the same time, Dr. Stainbrook has added a unique observation about poetry in the psychotherapeutic experience when he speaks of revitalizing and remoralizing the self. The reader will find that Dr. Stainbrook's chapter is a rare opportunity to sense the concept of experiential integration.

Dr. Charles Ansell follows with a psychoanalytic approach to poetry. He believes that in the convergence of psychoanalysis and poetry we have a unique and special means of understanding mystical experience as part of our daily lives.

Dr. Ken Edgar's chapter emphasizes a Jungian approach to poetry therapy. Dr. Edgar believes that poetry may be used as a tool in long-term treatment and thus be a part of a process which leads to a manifestation of the self to the self. What he proposes is to some extent comparable to Dr. Stainbrook's revitalizing and remoralizing the self and to Dr. Ansell's convergence of psychoanalysis and poetry.

The contribution of Dr. Robert N. Ross does not deal with therapy per se but is rather an effort to structure poetry into its linguistic components. Dr. Ross demonstrates that the patterns which emerge from these structures can provide therapeutic as well as linguistic information.

Dr. Owen E. Heninger, a psychiatrist who has been pioneering the use of poetry as a practical therapeutic tool in private practice, presents one case in depth. First he clarifies poetry as a treatment modality in uncovering unconscious forces. Then he shows how these forces can be organized into conscious, understandable meaning which can help an individual work through and deal with shattering emotional experiences.

Dr. Allan S. Abrams further emphasizes practical aspects of poetry therapy by considering his own therapeutic experiences in the proprietary psychiatric setting of Woodview-Calabasas Hospital. In so doing he shares with us his professional concerns and thus broadens our purview of a growing field.

Dr. Roger Lauer concentrates on safeguards in his chapter, "Abuses of Poetry Therapy." We are presented here with a realistic view of the professional who reminds us that poetry as a therapeutic intervention is also involved in ethical considerations. This reminder is most timely in view of the problems related to liability insurance, especially for individuals who engage in therapeutic endeavors without adequate supervision and training.

Acknowledging their debt to Dr. Moreno, the father of psychodrama, Dr. Gilbert A. Schloss and Dr. Dominick E. Grundy use the term "psycho-poetry" to focus on another dimension of experience in the field. They provide examples of action techniques, based on various conceptualizations, which offer a valuable and stimulating supplement to the poetry therapy process.

In presenting "Zen Telegrams," Mary Clancy and Dr. Roger Lauer address themselves to the fact that participants in poetry therapy groups may have doubts about moving from the real world to the world of imagination and revelation of feelings. The introduction of the Zen technique with its oriental connotation also suggests the potential of artistic techniques for poetry therapy which can be found in other cultures.

Louise Davis has worked with the editor for many years in using poetry as a therapeutic modality both at the Woodview-Calabasas Hospital and at the Poetry Therapy Institute. She explains why the paraprofessional in poetry therapy is of vital importance as part of a therapy team, and she points up the need for individuals who are knowledgeable in poetry and trained in therapy.

Dr. Julius Griffin, a prime mover in the organization of the Calabasas Hospital Neuropsychiatric Center and an early advocate in the use of bibliotherapy as a modality, is also a firm believer in the use of poetry in the therapeutic setting. His chapter is a natural outgrowth of his own professional understanding and development as well as a personal-practical history of his experiences in bibliotherapy.

Finally, Dr. Franklin M. Berry's chapter gets at the crux of the matter in any behavioral discipline—namely, what are your data and what do they mean. His "Approaching Poetry Therapy from a Scientific Orientation" is one of the first statistical studies in the field. The editor submits that this last chapter is in effect a closure pointing toward a new beginning which marks the coming of age of poetry therapy.

In conclusion, the editor would also like to finish where he began. The field of poetry therapy is at this time composed of diverging experiences and interests. As in Pirandello's *Six Characters in Search of an Author*, the various participants are searching for an author whose name may well be Dr. Inter-Discipline.

Arthur Lerner, Ph.D.

CHAPTER 1

Poetry and Behavior in the Psychotherapeutic Experience

Edward Stainbrook

Introduction

E. E. Cummings (1968) has suggested that

> *since feeling is first*
> *who pays any attention*
> *to the syntax of things*
> *will never wholly kiss you.* *

Yet poetry, like all culture, comes to life only in the behavior of people and then rarely as an experience of pure feeling alone. Indeed, such experiences as hysterical joy, abject despair, panic, or blind rage lack precisely the esthetically sensitive transformations, at once cognitive and linguistic, that are necessary for such feelings to become the behavior of poetry.

Poetic behavior, therefore, is that behavior which is evoked and maintained by the structure and process, by the cognition and imagery of a poem. It is, one may say, an esthetic organization which makes it possible for a person to feel his thoughts and imagery and to image and think his feeling. Mr. Cumming's complete kiss is in this experienced integration, in the wholeness of feelings full of thoughts and of thoughts full of feelings.

In the pursuit of an understanding of the behavior of poetry, therefore, we must not accept unwittingly the popular and long-held dichotomies of feeling-intellect, thought-emotion, or, even more broadly, irrational-rational. Even though in the evolution of animal behavior feeling was the first intelligence and determined the crucial decisions about acting or not acting, also present from the beginning was the sensing and perceiving of environmental information. For evolved and symbolizing man, cognition as image together with language and

---

*From "since feeling is first" in E. E. Cummings *Complete Poems 1913-1962*. Reprinted by permission of Harcourt Brace Jovanovich, Inc. and MacGibbon & Kee Limited/Granada Publishing Limited.

1

logic are inextricably interrelated with feeling. We have long known that much human suffering and impairment, individual and social, arise out of the imbalance or conflicts in the integration of feeling and cognition as adaptive, creative, or wholesome behavior in the human situation.

Our concerns here are specifically with the use of poetry in psychotherapy. Since all psychotherapy is based on various ideologies, theories, and techniques for arranging the interpersonal behavior of therapeutic experience, we must try to translate into the therapeutic context the influence on behavior of reading and hearing poetry. The creation of poetry may also be used in psychotherapy, but we shall not hope to encompass creative behavior in terms of our more limited concerns with the influences of already created poetry upon psychotherapeutic behavior.

Our objective, therefore, is to attempt to establish a comprehensive rationale which may guide the employment of poetry for the facilitation of behavioral changes sought in the processes and outcomes of psychotherapy. Initially, we shall attend to the sociocultural context of the psychotherapeutic process. We shall then turn to the personal interacting and interexperiencing of the participants. Finally, we shall examine the intrapersonal consciousness and subjectivity of the participant who is defined as the patient or client.

General Sociocultural Considerations

The overall structuring and control of psychotherapy in relation to hoped-for or predicted outcomes depends upon many variables determined by the process, the client, and the psychotherapist. The social structure and interactions of a therapeutic process are defined formally by a theory. In most cases the directing theory is only partially validated experimentally and in some situations may consist largely of unverified opinions and ideas. Every theory, ideology, or rationale of psychotherapy has a number of more or less clearly defined associated technical interventions or procedures. The use of poetry as a specific technical intervention should be based not only upon the behavioral implications of the immediate intervention but also upon a consideration of the total psychotherapeutic plan and process.

Considered as an experience with and between persons, psychotherapy is a temporary social relationship in which two or more persons intermittently come together to enact more or less well-defined social roles with one another. The behavior associated with the role of therapist is usually more clearly defined and less ambiguous than the role behavior of client or patient. This is largely due to previously learned professional behavior. Moreover, the client or patient has in most instances little or no prior training for enacting the role of patient. Indeed, bringing the behavior of the client under the control of the therapist's own conceptions and values of theory and experience, if that be an objective of therapy, depends largely on a collaborative detection and subsequent control of the client's role behavior as it relates to characteristics that are ambiguous or inappropriate in the ongoing psychotherapeutic relationship. In psychoanalysis, transference analysis is largely the study of role-inappropriate behavior in the client-therapist relationship.

Needless to say, the psychotherapist must be sufficiently aware and controlling of his own role behavior so that the ambiguous and inappropriate behavior of the client may be demonstrated convincingly and clearly. As a consequence, the client's behavior may be brought under more informed self-control and direction. With different theoretical implications, the need of the therapist for awareness and control of his own behavior (countertransference) is just as important for the social reinforcer role of the therapist in behavior modification as it is for the psychoanalyst.

The change or modification of specific behavior, defined by client or therapist as troublesome, trouble-making, deviant, unwanted, or symptomatic, is a major function and purpose of much psychotherapy. The utilization of poetry in therapy, however, should not be restricted by a preoccupation with the needs of "symptom-therapists" to concentrate upon the change of specific acts of behavior which may be thought to define the presence or absence of illness.

In a recent clarifying statement, Jerome Frank (1975) has elaborated a long-standing observation that it is not only, and sometimes not at all, specific symptoms which make a person seek help. It is rather his demoralization—a subjective sense of his failing ability to cope with himself in his present situation—which moves him to come to helping resources of all kinds, especially to psychotherapeutic agents.

The behavior that will be identified clinically as symptoms may be of variable importance as a cause of his demoralization. Indeed, some of the labeled symptoms may be the result of the client's own attempts to make his demoralization bearable and may be perceived and insistently maintained as gratifying.

Therefore, the essential needs of the client for the psychotherapeutic experience may not be expressed authentically in the symptomatic presentation of himself which formal entry into helping organizations and relationships may seem to demand. That is to say, feelings of loneliness, meaninglessness, and alienation from persons and culture may be presented as specifiable behavior (for example, depression, anxiety, resentment toward others), as some form of psychosomatic distress, or as the secondary consequences of various addictions. Or perhaps long-existing characteristic ways of behaving may be named as the now current problem. But for therapists to concern themselves only with symptom-clusters of behavioral acts, whether conceptualized primarily as thinking or as doing, is to ignore what is crucial in many cases—namely, that the client is demoralized because of the conditions of his existence and not necessarily because of acts defined as symptoms.

One could oversimplify by saying that there are therapies of specific symptoms and therapies of general personal demoralization. The adequate understanding of the effective therapeutic responses to demoralization requires, perhaps, a broader view of human behavior than may be necessary for the altering of specific symptomatic acts.

The tremendous importance to modern Western man of economic security and of the adequate access to material resources made the concept of economic deprivation a general model for the description of a faltering, unequal, or unfair environmental response to human needs other than those of basic survival. By extension, we speak easily in these times of social, cultural, and educational deprivation with the assumption that the necessary resources exist, at least potentially, and that the problems are essentially those of access and distribution to be solved by political action and social engineering. In a society of rapid change and inadequate organization for the creation and maintenance of interpersonal gratifications, many distressing and demoralizing individual situations arise out of the absence of intimate, gratifying, and enduring commitments to persons, institutions, and ideas. Such problems might also be talked about in terms of the deprivation of personally meaningful people and the lack of commitment to life-sustaining and life-enhancing activities and ideas. Hence, a most fundamental and growing threat to many persons is a sense of the loss of control of the purpose of life.

Unfortunately, meaning and purpose cannot be easily treated under an economic model as if they were temporarily absent or inaccessible resources. Progressively, more and more people in American culture and elsewhere are going to experience the loss of an absolute meaning and purpose. The cultural changes producing the present conceptual reality to which many people are now reacting have been going on for the last 200 years or more. Current scientific constructions of natural nature, of the physical world and of human nature, are diffusing widely and rapidly.

The resultant loss of religious and metaphysical absolutes may be considered as either diminishing or enhancing the human condition. Either science has killed God, or God is being inductively revealed by science. The brute fact, however, is that the absolutes of religious authority are no longer valid directives for contemporary living. But only by losing these absolutes of traditional meaning can one be free and hopeful in the creation of new relative alternatives. Sustaining relative truths cannot be created confidently until the "Absolute Truth" is relinquished.

It is in a society of rapid social change and of uncertain and relative meanings that the various psychotherapies and their practices are used by an increasing number of people in their search for the sense and meaning of their lives. It is also apparent that many of the so-called countercultural or revitalizing movements visible today are satisfying a human need to overcome a sense of alienation, powerlessness, and lack of meaning and to restore a sense of benign and responsive order and direction in the world. Some of these revitalizing movements, such as paranormal or extrasensory communication, meditation, enhancement of consciousness, and biofeedback, are friendly to scientific knowledge. Others, such as mysticism and astrology, are largely anti-scientific.

All these trends, along with the various Jesus movements, satisfy the needs of many people, particularly the young. The same needs are satisfied for an increasing number of others by the various psychotherapies, group or individual.

It is, perhaps, in these situations of existential despair that behavior evoked by the form and content of poetry and the other arts may be most significant in enhancing and potentiating the use of psychotherapy as a means of restoring a sense of purpose, self-direction, and self-control. Indeed, a recent essay in *Encounter* (1974), by the educational sociologist J. P. Ward, suggests there is a striking similarity between the sensitivity or training group structure and process and the Theater of the Absurd. In both, people are constrained by purely psychosocial considerations, arising within themselves as well as the situation, to remain in a human group experience convened by a leader who then abdicates leadership—a person in the group, God in the world. Because in Nietzsche's sense, man clings to the deceptions that make life tolerable, the group seeks to solve its dilemma by beginning to do tasks, to solve specific symptoms.

Perhaps an existential group therapy could be devised with the aid of poetic insight and outsight. Such a group could experience the leaderless situation, the meaningless world, from which there seems to be no escape but from which could be evolved a rebirth of self-determined meaning for the individual as well as the group. Such an outcome would occur not as a result of a defensive preoccupation with individual symptoms. It would arise in the form of collaborative decisions about what living is for, based on the group's encounter with the existential nakedness of social being and the recognition that authentic meaning arises out of a finite situational decision, not from the discovery of the Absolute.

Such a group experience would, perhaps, be seen as attractive by relatively few people. In the same sense, we might also say that psychoanalysis as an interpersonal, psychotherapeutic process is probably more productive but more selectively applicable when used for the development of enhanced and increased consciousness as against its more common use as a releaser from unconsciousness. Nevertheless, such speculation is suggestive of the increasingly fruitful merger of psychotherapy and poetry with its potential for formulating statements of existence and for structuring experiences out of which a revitalized and remoralized self may emerge.

All psychotherapy, therefore, will be characterized by some balancing of its attention between specific aspects of the help-seeker's behavior and his general sense of hope, meaning, confidence, and self-competence. Every helper must respond in some merger of healer and technician.

The Poetic Determination of Interpersonal Behavior

In considering the relation of poetry to psychotherapy just described, it is obvious that there can be no poetry therapy as such. As Dr. Arthur Lerner

(1973) has long insisted, poetry is a tool, a way of making a technical intervention into the structure and process of psychotherapy in order to enhance the emergence of a hoped-for result.

How, then, are we informed psychologically by poetry? Listening to or reading poetry is behavior. As a personal experience, we may want to keep the poetic encounter as spontaneous and uncomplicated by intellectual analysis as possible. But when we decide to use poetry technically to influence behavior in any situation at all, it then becomes necessary to have in mind a conceptual analysis of how poetry becomes behavior. We need some idea about what happens to the behaving person who is being informed by the poetry and whose experiencing is also at least partially organized and maintained by the psychosocial context of the reading or listening.

As we have already suggested, the participants engaged in psychotherapy are enacting social roles in which personal behavior is influenced by implicit and explicit expectations and assumptions as well as by the more or less rationally and technically prescribed character of interactive behavior enjoined by the therapy. There is a set of rules, varying in some respects from one form of therapeutic practice to another, for the expected and effective behavior of the participants. These rules, which in the first place may exist clearly only in the minds of therapists, establish the essential form, structure, and transactive processes of the relationship. They provide a baseline of interaction against which behavior can become visible, objectively as conduct or subjectively as awareness.

Like poetic and artistic productions in general, the psychotherapeutic undertaking has an overall formal structure. This shapes, controls, supports and potentiates the individual's experience so that the individual emerges from the therapeutic action, progressively and over a period of time, as an altered self. The outcome of the formal process is usually characterized by a reduction of existential and interpersonal distress and by some restoration of purpose, hope, self-esteem, self-control, competence, and effectiveness, with or without conspicuous alteration of specific behavior once identified as symptoms.

Therapists and clients, therefore, transact behavior with each other or, to blur somewhat the self-other separation, they create a human experience together within the form and meaning of the social process of psychotherapy. They also constitute among themselves the immediate environment in which experience is happening. Otto Rank (1941), one of the early nonmedical collaborators with Freud, once put very succinctly the essence of the psychoanalytic therapeutic transaction. It was a way, he said, of understanding the meaning of an interpersonal experience in the very act of having it.

The contributions of Freud and other psychoanalysts to an understanding of what is called transference and countertransference emphasize that for each participant this immediate environment of experiencing is always some individualized transformation of the existing interpersonal reality. Thus, to learn in psychodynamic therapies that one transforms cognitively the existing reality is to learn how to get free from old, outdated meanings and other retained reality-transformations which are informational deficits and distortions. As part of the same process, one also learns how to remain free in the play and work of creating new cognitive constructions of existence.

To borrow a concept from current mid-brow speech, the environment created by the psychotherapeutic group, be it dyadic or larger, is a temporary counterculture. When poetry is introduced into the group, the information of the poem is going to influence the reality of the participants' experience. This influence occurs in the psychotherapeutic environment in which the poem is being experienced; it happens at a particular time, in a particular subjective state, and in a particular psychosocial interactive context.

Poetry and Psychotherapeutic Role Behavior

Reading or listening to poetry either by oneself or in the special social context of psychotherapy is influenced, of course, by the general cultural assumptions about the meaning of poetry and by an individual's attitudes and characteristic reaction to poems. Most of us learn, formally or informally, that a poem is a special statement about the human condition produced by a person who creates and shapes a uniquely subjective experience into a culturally specified and meaningful mode of expression. A poem, therefore, can be considered as a culturally and esthetically organized exchange of being. If we attend to it at all, we do so with some assurance on the basis of our past experience and learning that it is part of an authentic cultural reality in which we may involve ourselves with various degrees of intensity.

Asking a participant in psychotherapy to read or listen to a poem immediately evokes a willingness to allow the information of the poetry to influence and determine his cognitive processes or his states and flow of consciousness. The desire and the readiness to surrender some control of his thinking to the structured and organized information of the poem is enhanced by the cultural authority attributed to the poem as a work of art. Moreover, the esthetic structuring of the poem invites the social role enactment of an empathetic identification with the imagery and thought of the poem. In his characteristic way the participant must identify with the poem and allow himself to behave as if the poem is his own thinking. In the words of Theodore Sarbin (1970), who has illuminated the general psychologic basis of imagining, the participant acts with more or less involvement to "hypothetically instantiate" or to attribute "as-if" reality to the experiencing suggested and structured by the poem.

In most psychotherapeutic countercultures or environments, expectations about behavior suggest explicitly or implicitly a liberation from the ordinary social restraints upon rationally directed and situationally focused behavior. Under such circumstances, the influence of the poem on the social behavior which occurs in psychotherapy reinforces the participant's shift to involvement in the cognitive processes of imagination. This is manifest in the form of diminished "defensive" and constricted thinking and an "as-if" involvement in the greater imaginative and experiential freedom of the poem. Moreover, the psychotherapeutic emphasis is usually on "getting in touch with feelings" and on the emergence into consciousness of out-of-awareness images and ideas. Hence, considerable reinforcement arises out of the therapeutic situation itself for itensifying the participant's identification and involvement with poetry, thereby enhancing the "as-if" instantiation of the poetically induced imagery. The cognitive freedom, urged as a psychotherapeutic attribute, also facilitates the participant's subjective role taking by means of which the poem is able to produce liberating and creative psychologic action without necessitating actual movement in the real world.

Poetry experienced in the psychotherapeutic context may result, therefore, not only in the most intense personal involvement with a poem but also in an effective psychotherapeutic resolution of distress and conflict.

But, as poetry therapists know, psychodynamic characteristics are highly relevant in determining the client's engagement with different poems and in determining the therapeutic value and relevance of specific poetry. Depending on both subjective and situational variables, poems differentially invite, repel, or simply do not engage high personal involvement in imaginative "as-if" behavior.

Lerner (1973), Rothenberg (1972), and many others have described aspects of poetic specificity and client conflict. As Rothenberg suggests, "Poets and psychotherapists are blood brothers" in the objectives of overcoming repression and in persuading the emergence of the "dispossessed consciousness" into self-awareness. Rothenberg, particularly, has stressed that in each poem the poet's expression and resolution of conflict and "the personal importance of phrases, images, ideas or metaphors felt but not conceived," which are the "soul-speech" of the poet, reverberate with the similar conflicts, anxiety, and distress of clients.

Consciousness, Cognition, Imagery, and Poetry

It seems obvious that once the conditions have been established in a psychotherapeutic setting under which the information and process of the poem are allowed to control significantly the cognitive behavior of a person, such behavior can then be used most effectively for the achievement of therapeutic goals.

In the 14th century one meaning of the verb "to inform" was the giving of conceptual form or shape to something discernible. But another more subtle meaning, also in frequent use at that time, was represented by the phrase "being informed" or "informing oneself." In agreement with contemporary information-processing models of brain and behavior, this second meaning can be appreciated as the shaping or forming of the subjective self. Information, thus conceived, literally makes form and processes in the brain and mind. One might say that experience, defined as information, structures and instructs behavior (even better, "instructures" behavior). Hence, one's self is literally a constantly changing integration of "instructures" which are being continuously reorganized by the thinking transformations of old and new experience.

This small excursion into word-history is to relate some aspects of an essentially cognitive, information-processing approach to an understanding of the functions of poetry in its evocation, maintenance, and modification of human behavior both within and outside the experience of psychotherapy. To invite participants in a psychotherapeutic process to read or attend to poetry is to allow their thinking behavior to be informed and directed for a time by the structure and content of a poem. If we assume that states of consciousness are determined by three basic components—namely, nervous structure, energy, and information—then reading or listening to poetry is a way of creating, directing, and maintaining thought processes and subjectively experienced consciousness.

What cognitive processes, particularly, are modulated by poetry? Since poetry therapy has usually found a more favorable reception among psycho-therapists allied with psychodynamic, phenomenologic, or existential theories, the poetic control of cognitive processes has been discussed largely in conceptual terms heavily influenced by psychoanalysis. Hence the cognitive processes of poetry are related to unconscious and preconscious mentation, primary process and dream thought, free association and creative regression. Rogers (1973) has recently formulated in these terms a somewhat condensed description of the imagining evoked by poetry: "Poetic imagery at its most creative moments mobilizes simultaneously a maximum amount of primary process mentation and an optimum amount of coordinate secondary process mentation, thereby generating a cluster of ideas in a vortex of emotional energy." Similarly, he succinctly defines one of the basic functions of poetic metaphor as expressing simultaneously both the meaning of the intentional and of the repressed. Using this conceptualization, poetry may be viewed as one way of facilitating the emergence of primary process thinking into consciousness and communicable thought.

However, such a statement is an inadequate representation of the poetically determined cognition occurring in therapy. To begin with, the primary-secondary process model is too undifferentiated for effective use in the contemporary psychophysiology of thinking. In addition, such a model is concerned almost entirely with the transformation of the unconscious into consciousness. The emphasis is on learning how not to be unconscious.

Our present concerns and interests must be much more in the direction of enhancing or creating and forming more consciousness—that is, of not only emphasizing how to be less "unconscious" but of learning to be more conscious. What is conceptualized as unconscious in psychoanalytically based models refers to any genetically created neurostructures and their intrinsic cognitive content or functions plus what was once conscious experience but is now repressed. Yet, much of the enhancement and differentiation of consciousness consists of learning and experiencing what has never before occurred. The learning of consciousness is achieved both retrospectively and prospectively.

An invitation to imagine and to evoke the imagery of experience by linguistic symbolization and metaphor is an essential characteristic of poetic communication. Therefore, the general psychology of cognition is highly relevant, particularly the functions of imagery as a mode of processing information and of representing, storing, transforming, and communicating experience. Such a source may be more helpful for an understanding of the use of poetry to influence therapeutic behavior than are the polarizing concepts of primary and secondary process thinking.

Largely from a developmental point of view, Jerome Bruner (1966) has suggested that cognition might be described usefully in terms of three interrelated representational systems. First, in agreement with Piaget but not with Freud (who assumed that hallucinatory imagery preceded action), Bruner speaks of the "enactive" mode of cognitive representation in which action and cognitive consciousness are essentially the same. Thinking is action and memory is remembered action.

A second system of representation may be called the "iconic." Horowitz (1970) prefers to label it image thinking, emphasizing the various sensory organizing subsystems which contribute the visual, auditory, and other sensory components of the complex and simultaneous imagined integrations of experiencing.

The cognitive skills and functions that develop with the learning of language and with the ability to describe, order, and think about experience by using words, syntax, and logic are called by Bruner the "symbolic," and by Horowitz the "lexical" mode of thought representation.

Dream thinking is characterized by its relative overemphasis on the enactive and iconic modes of representation, and conscious self-reflective thought demonstrates the increased awareness of imagery in the background of conscious lexical thinking. Thus, the content of consciousness, asleep and awake, displays the interrelation among these various modes—enactive, iconic, and lexical—of the cognitive processing of experiencing.

Language and linguistic behavior can be considered as informational coding added to action and imagery. Imagery and action can, of course, be experienced without any verbal or lexical behavior at all. The iconic and enactive modes of cognition can also be the predominant and major modes of expression, and verbal communication and the accompanying lexical information may remain covert and suppressed. With particular reference to poetry, the lexical linguistic mode may be used to restore the originality of action and imagery to the culturally desiccated or psychologically impoverished word by using language as a code to evoke a totality of experiencing and to turn the lexical token of an experience into its whole.

In this latter use the language of poetry functions restoratively and psychotherapeutically by enhancing consciousness with the enactive and imaginal responses of persons to their past and present experiences. This aspect of experiencing is what the ordinary language of living short-circuits and suppresses.

It is here that we must turn again to the main point of our discussion, which is to relate an essentially cognitive and information-processing approach to the function of poetry as it evokes, maintains, and modifies human behavior within a psychotherapeutic process. We have seen that this tripartite relationship (balancing cognition, psychosocial behavior, and therapeutic process) enables us to view poetry as a therapeutic intervention, not restricted to specific acts or to the symptomatic treatment of these acts. We have also seen that poetry as intervention is adjunctive to the general therapeutic outcome of restoring self-direction and self-control to the client. Finally, and perhaps most important, there exists the possibility that in its optimum potential the merger of poetry with therapy may result in the revitalizing and remoralizing of the self by providing a wholeness of consciousness—an integration of emotion, cognition, and imagery—with which to create and maintain personal meaning.

References

Bruner, Jerome S., Olver, Rose R., & Greenfield, Patricia M. *Studies in cognitive growth.* New York: Wiley, 1966.

Cummings, E. E. *Complete Poems: 1913-1962.* New York: Harcourt Brace Jovanovich, 1968. P. 208.

Frank, Jerome D. "An overview of psychotherapy." In Gene Usdin (Ed.), *Overview of the psychotherapies.* New York: Brunner-Mazel, 1975. Pp. 3-21.

Horowitz, Mardi Jon. *Image formation and cognition.* New York: Appleton-Century-Crofts, 1970.

Lerner, Arthur. "Poetry therapy." *American Journal of Nursing,* 1973, *73*, 1336-1338.

Rank, Otto. *Beyond psychology.* Camden, N.J.: Haddon Craftsmen, 1941.

Rogers, Robert. "On the metapsychology of poetic language: Modal ambiguity." *The International Journal of Psycho-Analysis,* 1973, *54*, 61.

Rothenberg, Albert. "Poetic process and psychotherapy." *Psychiatry,* 1972, *35*, 228-254.

Sarbin, Theodore R., & Juhasz, Joseph B. "Toward a theory of imagination." *Journal of Personality,* 1970, *38*, 52-76.

Ward, J. P. "The T-group." *Encounter,* 1974, *42*, 30-40.

CHAPTER 2

Psychoanalysis and Poetry

Charles Ansell

On the face of it the juxtaposition of psychoanalysis and poetry may seem more literary invention than the product of thoughtful study, but the facts prove otherwise. Sigmund Freud, the founder of psychoanalysis, was deeply involved with the special nature of the creative mind. He admired the creative artist tremendously. He frequently described his awe at the powerful insights of the great artists he revered. His paper on Michelangelo's Moses, his views of Dostoevsky, his continuing fascination with Shakespearean heroes and the works of the early Greek dramatists, all contributed substantially to the awesome development of psychoanalytic psychology.

The teacher of psychoanalysis may feel hard put to choose which of Freud's major contributions to psychoanalysis was the most important. The entire field of psychoanalysis would have to include Freud's monumental work on dreams, his very original views on the theory of mind, his clear delineation of pathological states, his views of psychosexual development, and his additional gifts in articulating a treatment modality. Freud has made other contributions, but for our immediate purpose his larger views of the unconscious constitute our principal concern in this chapter on the relation between psychoanalysis and poetry.

Each of these major currents of psychoanalytic theory has been made the subject of lively interest. Most recently the ego, the portion of mind described by Freud as the conscious perception of self, has moved into a central position of importance. The philosopher or the social historian might attempt to explain why of all the major currents in psychoanalytic theory, the ego has commanded the greater attention. One might speculate that the ego, with its promise of mastery over the unknown unconscious, becomes an enormously important social tool for control and redirection of our flooding impulses.

But this drift toward the development of an ego psychology carries certain consequences. It tends to deemphasize the larger scope of the unconscious and hence to deprecate our efforts at understanding our human heritage. "Human heritage may seem a curious term to illuminate the scope and content of our unconscious. At this point in our knowledge of the unconscious, we have only the barest of clues to suggest that there is an earlier-than-birth source of our unconscious. We are not quite done with the issue of the *tabula rasa* versus racial memory. One view holds that the human slate of experience is clean at birth, unmarked by any trace of former lives imbedded in a transmitted unconscious. The other view hints at the presence of a primordial state of consciousness, a quality of unconscious passed from generation to generation which carries memory traces, flashes of *deja vu*, etc.

It is not our purpose here to enter into metapsychological inquiries into the unconscious. Our purpose is rather to examine the nature of the unconscious, to search for clues which might explain the mysterious symbols that appear in our dreams, that sometimes appear in trance states, and that more frequently appear as poetic idioms.

The poem and the unconscious share a major feature: both are represented in compressed form. The dream images themselves are by now known to be elaborately complicated symbolizations of various thoughts, wishes, fears. Thus, a young woman troubled over the possibility of an unwanted pregnancy dreamed she walked along the banks of the Ganges River in India. She wore the traditional sari and gazed pensively at the quiet waters. Out of her long chain of associations to arrive at the hidden meaning of the dream she spoke of *Mother India*, a book title then popular. She spoke of the Biblical river which carried the child Moses to Pharoah's daughter. The joinder of the Ganges River in India with the association to Moses as the abandoned infant seemed to compress not only the fact of her imminent motherhood, but also her doubts about its timeliness in her life.

We live our life in symbols. We look out at sunset, at a tree, and believe that what we see corresponds to a scientific description of the natural world. We believe that every other human being who looks out on the world of nature believes with certainty that we all behold the same thing. Early philosophers struggled with the question of our reliability as observers. Some, like Plato, argued that the real world was concealed from us and that what we beheld was but subjective impressions. He drew a parable of several people sitting inside a cave, their backs against the mouth of the cave. In this position they could only see the shadow of things passing outside of the cave as they were reflected on the wall of the cave facing them. Those seated inside the cave would insist that the shadows were the reality of things observed. In this view we are all looking out on the world and see only the shadows of whatever reality exists. Immanuel Kant struggled with this issue and finally declared that everything in the world of nature carried its own reality, "the-thing-in-itselfness," which could be dramatically different than our perception of it.

How much more difficult then becomes the matter of establishing the reality of a mood, a reaction to words spoken. In the end, we are forever creating personal meanings out of our chosen ways of perceiving experience. When one person looks out at a sunset and observes the striking colors in the sky above, his impressions of the scene, the mood it creates in him, the thoughts it evokes are far more pertinent to his characteristic way of perceiving the world than a scientist's explanation of light refraction. We move through our lives projecting our perceptions of events on experience and we insist that we are observers of a universal reality.

At bottom, we are all of us constantly recreating the world. If there were a universal sameness, a universal reality to things in nature, we would walk through life with the brute indifference of a frog hopping on the bank of a river.

Only the poet knows in a very special way that perception is the artist's principal gift. With perception he can shape and reshape all manner of experience. He can carry his perception forward and backward on a time track, capture the perceptions of childhood and restate them as an adult. And when we read the poet's rendering of his perceptions, we are often struck with the shock of recognition of a long forgotten moment in our own lives.

Perceptions, then, are private judgments of experience. There may be universal agreement on viewing the natural world, but our views here are of the grossest character. The closer we draw to the objects in the natural world, through our microscopes and our telescopes, the more our view changes. A judgment, then, of objects in nature depends upon the degree of scrutiny we employ in studying the object. Hence, views change as our viewing mechanisms change.

In our normal life with people, more than in our life with objects of nature, our views change with our changing judgments. Thus, the judgments we may have of certain experiences could change under changed circumstances. What, then, can we say of all those judgments we now hold which shape our lives? We may well, on this basis, call all of our judgments into question, and give them the name of "illusion." The dictionary defines illusion as "A perception which fails to give the true character of an object perceived." This definition of illusion might well serve to define "delusion," which is generally understood to mean such a derangement of view that we count the observer to be suffering from some mental strain.

What we are saying here is that our perceptions of our experiences cannot "give the true character of an object perceived" and we are all, therefore, locked in a system of illusion which we swear to be true and in accord with nature. The thought that we live our daily lives directing our speech and our behavior through a network of illusions may earn quick disapproval from many persons. It is obviously important to us that our views of our experiences are not only regarded as normal in the sense that most would unhesitatingly agree with our perceptions, but that our views are correct and in such conformity with reality that even the tree itself, if it could speak, would agree that our perception of it is correct. This view of ourselves in the world, whether in the world of nature or the world of persons, is psychologically important if we are to feel secure in our ability to function and move among our fellow humans.

The psychoanalyst and the poet, each in his own way, understand the central role illusion plays in our lives. The psychoanalyst knows that we pass through our lives encountering a succession of experiences and that we assign our own unique meanings to experience. When we love and when we hate, when we grow angry and when we feel compassionate depends entirely on our particular view of the experience before us. It would be foolhardy to assert that certain vital experiences which we encounter in our lives carry within themselves the clear character of comedy or tragedy. Experiences in and of themselves are neither comic nor tragic, neither wrath provoking nor sorrowful. An event becomes an experience when we choose to give it our highly personal meaning. To be sure, we are expected to be sad at funerals and happy at weddings, but these are socially contrived events in which we share a gross and superficial sameness of reaction. But when we speak of ultimate meaning, it is doubtful that we share in drawing the same ultimate meaning from such experiences.

Thus, the psychoanalyst understands that when we protest the experiences in our lives, when we insist that family members and friends are hurting us, we are perhaps crying out from the pain of a far earlier reading of experience in our lives, perhaps out of the pains of our early childhood. These early pains fix themselves in our consciousness and serve as a model for future experiences. We tend to repeat early learned meanings in later experiences. Thus, to continue to believe that we are under attack is to live within an illusion. It is, after all, a perception of experience of which William Blake, that poet of the darkness of soul, once wrote:

> To the Eyes of a Miser a Guinea is more beautiful than the Sun & a bag worn with the use of Money has more beautiful proportions than a Vine filled with Grapes. The tree which moves some to tears of joy is in the Eyes of others only a Green thing that stands in the way. . . . As a man is So he Sees. (Erdman, 1965, p. 676)

Poets have known for centuries that a man is as he sees. Illusion, then, is the stuff of our lives. Those who not only know this, but who are eternally restless in searching for ever richer meanings beneath our illusions, are the poets of the world.

* * *

The poet, more than the historian captures the hidden essence of the civilization in which he lives. The historian captures the upper thoughts of his time, those thoughts and significances that are at hand in documents and in state papers. The poet moves through a hidden world. His uncoverings lay beneath the conventional wisdom of his time. Thus, there is a vast difference between the poet and the historian, a difference marked from the earliest of times by two major myth systems, each of which has contributed to the development of human society.

The historian's tradition perhaps began with the early Greeks and their love of knowledge. That knowledge which Socrates, Plato, and Aristotle spoke of was, in today's terms, an experience in rational inquiry. Their fascination lay in the ceaseless wondering over man's reliability as an observer of natural phenomena. I had said earlier that Plato regarded the human as a fatally limited observer of natural phenomena. At the core of Greek thought was a view of man in his world which would impel him into wider and deeper searching into his surroundings. It seemed a quiet madness to invade the natural world and lay bare its secrets. The principle of cause and effect as it played itself out in the natural world laid a foundation for the rise of Western thought and, ultimately, Western civilization.

The Greeks with their passion for knowledge eventually led the Western world into a new freedom, the freedom to view nature unencumbered by an earlier view of demonic magic and extraterrestrial spirits. The new freedom led to new visions of society. It released new energies that led to technological advances, to the rise of cities, and to the formation of democratic governments. Rational thought processes opened up new sciences. The central myth of freedom to inquire celebrated the idea of Truth, but this Truth was regarded as rational by science and technology and was thereafter limited to those findings that could claim obvious correspondence with nature. Truth rested on verification, and verification demanded that all who observed the same phenomena arrive at a consensus. Truth in a rational world could not suffer uncertainty.

Freedom to inquire and the truth of verification captured the upper meaning of events. The advances of freedom and truth made knowledge an end in itself. The answers which a freedom based on rational inquiry could yield were necessarily free of symbols or hidden meanings. A symbol, as we have said earlier, serves as a compression of meanings, often mixed and sometimes contradictory.

As time passed, a widening gap grew between those who sought knowledge for knowledge sake and those who sought for meanings more distant than science could yield, more hidden than a rational view could accept. Kierkegaard long ago despaired of the rising cult of the scientific spirit that stopped short of delving into the mysteries of man's spirit, that turned away from searching among the divine spheres. Kierkegaard viewed the intellectual of his time as detached and impersonal, frozen in a posture forced on him by the study of an objective environment. The knowledge seeker for Kierkegaard was adrift in a rudderless craft and did not know that he was lost. Directions, goals, ultimate meanings were not within the concern of the scientific truth seeker.

The gap between those who studied nature objectively and those who viewed it subjectively grew wider until, like two parts of a mainland, they were cut apart and sent drifting away from each other. Those who wonder over the inner meaning of events may be found far earlier in man's history than the later knowledge seekers. Early man expressed his wisdom in fables, in parables, in myths. They were repeated over generations, over long stretches of time, and ultimately found their way into religious literature. The myths that spoke of hidden meanings became the very heart of the great religious systems, East and West. These were fables and myths that could not be found within one major work or in any given set of writings. They grew out of several cultures and were created over a length of time. Mainly they were fables and parables that told of the wonders in the universe. They told of giant passions loose in the universe, passions that moved men either to great heights or to their ruin. They were filled with celebrations of great lords of creation that watched over man, warning him, guiding him, rewarding him, punishing him.

Beneath the fables and parables lay man's never ending search for meaning. How could the meaning of the universe be found in the final formula of $E=mc^2$? How could the meaning of life itself be found in a modern work on scientific psychology? Karl Marx, writing from an altogether different view, posed the same question. In an attack upon the philosophers of his time he cried out that the point in all knowledge was not to describe the world but to change it. Marx, like Kierkegaard earlier, chided the mandarins of knowledge for their vainglorious posturing as wise men. Though widely different from each other's outlook, both men, Kierkegaard and Marx, sought for meanings and directions beneath the accumulated store of knowledge. One was driven by a passion for religious faith, the other was propelled by a politically revolutionary fervor to establish his vision of Utopia. Both shared a common zeal for ultimate values which could ennoble mankind.

Thus, the passions of vast dreams and great ideals separated from the cool detachment of objective inquiry. The one searched deep in the hidden world to find meanings; the other gazed outward to the world with notebook and instruments. The poet engages his very being as the principal instrument of discovery. His work becomes his notations.

One might well wonder how a civilization could so separate the two perspectives and yet remain hospitable to each? The poet and the scientist yield their work to society, yet each speaks in tongues sometimes unfamiliar to the other.

Were we to allegorize this duality of views, we would find no more strangely suitable model than man's own life as a human being. Man's need to survive compelled him to understand and conquer the natural world. His creature needs for food, clothing, and shelter led him into a view of his world that of necessity required him to master the errant and unpredictable in nature. Man became an instrument of knowledge. He recorded events, he measured distances, he learned practical and efficient methods to live within the natural world.

Though he always knew (if only vaguely) the parables and fables that informed his society, he separated himself from their dominion over him and gave himself over to studying the knowable. To continue our allegory, man the rational seeker after verifiable truths appeared to succeed in shutting himself off from the large scale passions expressed in the great myths and fables of earlier times. Man the knowledge seeker, the formalizer of science, the objective detached wanderer on earth emerged in the personification of the Freudian ego. As the ego measures its strength by the accuracy of its perceptual functions (reality testing) and by the successful repression of impulses that might hinder perceptual clarity, so rational man (rational ego) trained his observational skills to deliver observations with unerring accuracy.

This view of the ego describes man as a disciplined observer, careful to guard against contaminants which might impair his accuracy. It is a necessary caution, for the secrets of the natural world are not surrendered to fools and dreamers. But it is also a limiting discipline, for now man was shut off from the passions that once lived at the center of the myths and fables, that gave rise to the great religions, and gave man a thirst for the divine. No matter that the fables and parables seemed childish or fancied nonsense, they were the great evocations that rose out of man's cry for meaning.

Thus, we come to the great unknowable—man's unconscious. It is on this great stage where passions raged, where dreams unfolded, and where an ancient restlessness wandered freely. Here poets roam freely and listen for echoes that may have been voices that once stirred men to passions beyond their understanding. The myth, the dream, remains the secret code and the parables remain the language that hints at hidden meanings.

Groddeck, an early psychoanalyst, once said of the dream, "We are dreamed." The dream that rises out of our unconscious pauses before us without our conscious will. It plays itself out in a life of its own. But its meanings still elude us. In his monumental work on dreams Freud charted a labyrinth over which impulses traveled over time, dipping into the present for fresh representation, but always hearkening back to a distant past where early wishes, though hinted, were never truly forgotten. For Freud, the unconscious was the void, the chaos before the creation. There was no order, no awareness of time or place—only brute demands borne on the back of an animal heritage.

Freud prided himself as a scientific investigator. He sought to impress his medical contemporaries that psychoanalysis was a science. In elaborating his metapsychological theories he took pains to chart out paths where emotions traversed. He drew diagrams to suggest the positions of different sections of the mind. And when ego psychology gained wide popularity, the unconscious seemed tame and entirely conquerable.

Modern ego psychology, in American psychoanalytic circles particularly, appears to have entered the ranks of the rational knowledge seekers. The truth that science sought seems closer at hand to ego psychology, for here behavior is conceptualized within a pattern that begins with an impulse from the unconscious and is effectively transformed by the ego into acceptable behavior via a defense system developed by the "maturing" ego.

* * *

For millenia, the early poets and myth makers, the prophets from the world's religious teachings, have touched the shores of an unexplored wisdom hidden in our unconscious. Their insights burst like flashes of light in some darkness. They spoke in verse, in proverbs, in parables. They did not build complete systems of thought brick on brick. They did not so much speak as they were spoken. It was as Groddeck has said of dreams. Their dark wisdom broke out in myths and parables. They rose unwilled from some depths in their lives.

The unconscious does not seek knowledge; it seeks meanings. Its expressions have become our art forms. The mysterious glare in Michelangelo's Moses, the ascending counterpoint in a Bach fugue, the dark passions of Milton's *Paradise Lost*, are all profound evocations rising out of the artist. They live in our minds not as statements as clear as a revered historical document but as a comment on existence which each of us feels as a very personal message intended only for us.

We come now to a brief glimpse at the early history of pre-modern myth makers, the mystics and poets whose spirit and messages entered the heart of later civilizations. The separation of the poet and the mystic from the world of knowledge seekers is a comparatively recent phenomenon. In pre-Christian times, in the ancient worlds of Greece, Rome, and Judea, and in Persia, India, and China, men rose out of limiting civilizations in which they lived and spoke of awesome visions. Their visions seemed startlingly new for their times. And though each of these mystics lived a lifetime in isolated cultural communities, barely traveling beyond the borders of their familiar worlds, they burst forth with insights and world views never before heard in their time and place.

In ancient Judaic civilization Abraham pursued a vision dramatically different from his forebearers. When he broke from his father's faith of idol worship, he moved physically and spiritually away. He left behind his father's house to go up to a new and strange land. He left the only form of worship known to him and his father before him to choose a new God, an abstract God idea, no longer visible as an idol. It was a transcendental moment in man's history; for in Abraham's "discovery" of monotheism, he laid the groundwork for a revolutionary perception of man to himself. If man could pursue a God no longer external in the natural world, then it would be a God created entirely out of man's own inner spiritual endowments. Man's communications with his God would undergo profound transformations. The pagan ceremonies of earlier idol worshippers, the pagan rites of animal and human sacrifices, were now to be abandoned in favor of mystical devotionals and celebrations of miracles which only a universal, omnipotent God could perform. The devotionals became the poetic psalms composed by men who felt deeply moved by inner visions of the new God created in man's image. The call to search one's inner spirit became the great prophecies of Isaiah.

Elsewhere in the ancient world other men rose with great visions, men strange to each other and strange too to the civilizations from which they sprang. Confucius and Lao Tse rose out of ancient China. The Buddha came out of ancient India. Homer rose out of ancient Greece to pen the great epic poems of great spirits. Each mind proclaimed a new vision far grander and more sweeping in the breadth of its wisdom than any voice heard before. Each of these great spirits from ancient civilizations—from Judea, from Greece, from China, and from India—bore witness to a historical time when men could transcend their time and place. It was as Earl Jaspers has written, an axial age, a time of transcendence. To transcend is to stand back and look beyond in a hitherto unknown mode of being in which one questions reflectively one's actual world and struggles to attain a new vision of what lies beyond. To attain that state, Buddha renounced princely possessions, Confucius sought the source of *jen* within; Lao Tse yearned for the Tao.

Transcendence as idea is foreign to modern scientific psychology, but not foreign to those psychological schools of thought that view man as living in a continuing state of awareness. The philosophically minded student views transcendence as dramatic movement in the never ending human experience of becoming. The poet struggles to transcend himself. He dares to press against the barriers of the experiencing mind, to enter into states of being in which new visions and more far-reaching vistas of life's meaning may unfold.

It is perhaps a commonplace to observe that all creative art is an experience in transcendence. Psychologically, art which transcends the experience witnessed by the mind presses deeper into states of feeling not immediately accessible to consciousness. In the clinical language of psychoanalysis, the so-called contents of the unconscious often emerge as derivatives of early instinctual impulses. As derivatives when they emerge into consciousness they appear in behavioral forms, quite removed from their early pre-socialized contents. Thus, the world of the unconscious in clinical psychoanalysis belongs to the *it* in us, for to the psychoanalyst we become an *I* after we have effectively conquered the wayward nature of the unconscious and after we have learned conventional modes and ideas acceptable to the I's of other selves.

Thus, there appear to be two different views of the unconscious. For the clinically minded, the unconscious, like formless clay, waits on experience to give it shape. Only that portion of the unconscious is relevant that is deemed vital for life's main purposes. The so-called sexual instincts wait for an eventual channeling into the social expectancies. We learn to love tenderly and marry wisely. We reproduce ourselves and rear our children intelligently. Our ego instincts are soon trained to accept the "reality" principle which vouchsafes us a life free of unnecessary risks and dangers. When we have effectively directed our sexual instincts in accord with societal standards and when we have demonstrated a necessary caution and prudence in the conduct of our daily lives, we may be said to have mastered the brute forces of the unconscious and harnessed its energies to peaceful and productive pursuits.

There is, however, another view of the unconscious, one which we have touched upon earlier. I refer to the hidden world of our lives. Though hidden, it is a world continually under siege by the restless poet. Under this view, the poet does far more than transform the naked thrust of instinctual impulses. He transcends an early self. Under this view, we part company from the traditional clinician largely because we have entered upon areas more mystical than speculative. Nietzsche once wrote: "The poet presents his thoughts festively, on the carriage of rhythm; usually because they could not walk."

Other thinkers have attempted to capture the transcendent mood of the poet as he delivers hitherto unheard thoughts into universal recognition. William James spoke of varieties of religious experience. Freud visited the classical world of the Italian Renaissance in a mood bordering on mystical reverence. Carl Jung acknowledged states of feeling which the great religious prophets knew and recorded for us. Each of us in our time has known moments that filled us with a strange sense of being, which seemed to lift us out of a familiar place into the presence of a new spirit beyond any we have known.

Is it possible to capture these luminous moments and hold them up to close examination? It is a feat already accomplished by many men over many centuries. They are to be found in sublime paintings, in the epic poems, in the penetrating insights of Shakespeare, Milton, Blake. Are these magnificent expressions no more than transformations of early instinctual impulses?

It may be helpful to repeat here our earlier view of the human mind in its division between the spheres of consciousness and the boundless unconscious to stand as a paradigm with two civilizations, the ancient and the modern. The modern period in this paradigm corresponds to states of consciousness in its major dependence on belief systems based on verifiable knowledge. The other, a still undiscovered universe, corresponds to ancient civilizations where belief systems rose from transcendental experiences. To state the matter sharply, the moderns have elevated consciousness. In consequence the unconscious has not only thus been subordinated but is often made to appear as a menace to the cleansing functions of the conscious mind. Clearly, in this view the unconscious suffers massive constriction. It is a view that dismissed the unknowable either as the immature cries of a pleasure-seeking infant or as a vast network of aborted dreams and idle visions.

Thus, the two views come into collision. One celebrates reason, a quality of reason that must emerge as pure and clear as a mathematical equation; the other moves restlessly through areas of human experience that seem beyond charting and map making. A noted scholar recently observed that "religions prosper in the absence of theology; they often die from too much theology." Religion in this context suggests feelings for the divine which spread out over our very existences. Theology defines and hence limits religion. Similarly, reason defines and hence limits experience. The unconscious, the eluder of reason, moves through a boundless universe of experience. All art must in the end make its home in the unconscious of our lives.

* * *

We have thus far been urging the thesis that the true source for the poetic imagination is in the unconscious. We have said that the ego as a frame of mind has a principal responsibility to assess reality and to respond appropriately to that reality. Seen in this light the ego appears to be an anemic participant in the creative process. To thus characterize the ego as weak in the process of creation leaves us with the problem of identifying the voice of the unconscious. To say that the authentic source for the creative process lies in our unconscious and then deny the ego any function in serving as the voice of the unconscious is to suggest that the poet drifts into a trance state to circumvent the ego. Clearly, such a view of the ego's role in the creative process fails to explain how the unconscious is made conscious in the creative process.

Another view of the ego, psychoanalytically, is essential if we are to bridge the gap between the vague, transcendental stirrings of the unconscious and the ego function of making all self-feelings intelligible. The new image of the ego, the ego that serves the poet to communicate his transcendent experience, can ill afford to endure the stressful anxieties that may have in past times usurped the full attention of the ego, leaving it too troubled to experience creative introspection. The ego of the poet must first be free of those imperious drives that propel most of us to fit comfortably in the world. The psychic reader of another's unconscious is expected to empty himself of anxious thoughts if he would make contact with the other's unconscious.

The "mind" of the poet is both open and empty. It is open to free introspection, open to direct communication with his unconscious and empty of the distractions of those anxieties that propel most of us into preformed modes of thinking and feeling. Buber hints at this necessary frame of mind, open to the novel and empty of the "preconcerted," if human encounter is to be creative. The ego state after a thoroughgoing psychoanalysis may be said to be free of the anxieties that life sets down on our path. The anxieties of the Western mind are imbedded in the drives toward wide acceptance by a society prizing conformity as the price of approval.

We speak here not of a conformity of taste and dress but of a conformity that teaches us how to feel negatively and positively. This latter conformity, however ambiguous and vague, is nevertheless a continuing experience in desire and frustration largely because our ego is a dependent self, waiting constantly for signals that spell approval from disapproval. But to the unified and accepted self (ego), the truth is that the more ourselves we are, the less self is in us.

The analyzed ego, though not deliberately trained for a creative life, becomes a gift to the talented. It is a gift because it bestows freedom, and with freedom it endows a courage to express all that lies hidden within us.

We come at last to a genuine convergence between psychoanalysis and poetry. Psychoanalysis is exploration in depth. It acknowledges the presence of the unconscious, but it also knows that by itself the unconscious cannot rise freely to the surface of consciousness, into the domain of the ego. Psychoanalysis knows that a state of tension exists between the unconscious and the ego, a tension that some observers ascribe to the lifelong struggle between the drive to self-actualization and the overweening pressure of instinctual impulses for immediate gratification. Psychoanalysis encourages the ego to sift among the crowding impulses, to discriminate among the demands, to set aside mindless gratifications. In the end psychoanalysis liberates the ego by placing the host of instinctual impulses at the service of the ego.

The ego of which we now speak is not the ego of ego psychology, but an ego that acknowledges the unconscious from which it has sprung and to which it remains associated in active and alert states. The school of psychoanalytic thought that perceives the ego as born fully grown, endowed with its own unconscious, and destined to bend its unconscious into adaptive behavior would cut the human mind free of a great source of riches in man's capacity to transcend himself. The ego of which we speak weds the unconscious with itself and delivers symbols and illusions that touch the depths of human experiencing.

It is this ego that maintains itself in a state of awareness of stirrings and intimations that may have been borne by millenia of other unconscious existences in time. It seems ironic that psychoanalysis, this century's greatest contribution to the scientific study of human thought and human behavior, should be the vehicle that elevates the mystical in humankind to the plane of the familiar. For, in the final analysis, to liberate the ego of worldly anxieties is to unlock a door closed far too long.

References

Buber, Martin. *Between man and man.* London: Routledge & Kegan Paul, New York: Macmillan, 1947.

Erdman, David V. (Ed.) *The poetry and prose of William Blake.* Garden City, N.Y.: Doubleday, 1965.

Ellenberger, Henri F. *The discovery of the unconscious.* New York: Basic Books, 1970.

Fingarette, Herbert. "The ego and mystic selflessness." *Psychoanalysis and Psychoanalytic Review*, Spring-Summer 1958, 5-39.

Freud, Sigmund. *The interpretation of dreams.* New York: Basic Books, 1955.

Freud, Sigmund. "Formulations regarding the two principles in mental functioning" (1911). In *Collected papers*, IV: 13-21. *Papers on metapsychology; papers on applied psycho-analysis.* Edited by Ernest Jones, No. 10. London: Hogarth Press and the Institute of Psycho-Analysis, 1950.

Freud, Sigmund. "A note on the unconscious in psycho-analysis" (1912). In *Collected papers*, IV: 22-29. Edited by Ernest Jones, No. 10. London: Hogarth Press and the Institute of Psycho-Analysis, 1950.

Freud, Sigmund. "The unconscious" (1915). In *Collected papers*, IV: 98-136. Edited by Ernest Jones, No. 10. London: Hogarth Press and the Institute of Psycho-Analysis, 1950.

Frye, Northrop. "The critical path." *Daedalus*, Spring 1970, 268-342.

Groddeck, Georg. *The book of the it.* New York: Funk & Wagnalls, 1950.

Laing, R. D. *The divided self.* London: Tavistock, 1960.

Schwartz, Benjamin I. "The age of transcendence." *Daedalus*, Spring 1975, 1-7.

Weil, Eric. "What is a breakthrough in history?" *Daedalus*, Spring 1975, 21-36.

Wyss, Dieter. *Psychoanalytic schools.* New York: Aronson, 1973.

CHAPTER 3

The Epiphany of the Self
Via Poetry Therapy

Ken Edgar

The hypothesis of this study is that the epiphany of the self may be observed in long-term treatment of patients in poetry therapy. Analysis of the poems submitted by patients over a period of time suggests the validity of the Jungian concept (Jung, 1953) that the self may emerge in a hierarchy, from child to hero to self. Radin (1948) elaborated upon this Jungian concept with his observation that human growth may follow distinct cycles: subsequent to the child, the emergence of trickster, transformer, Red Horn, and the Twins, all of which is part of the epiphany of the self. This would mean that an individual would evolve from child through the four phases of hero: the trickster hero (playing tricks), the transformer hero (doing good), the Red Horn hero (physical courage), and finally the hero with the twin values of wisdom and warmth. The self at this point would begin to emerge.

In poetry therapy many patients will evolve through this same sequence, and growth can be observed in the projections of the poetry. First of all, however, the patient tends to displace *symptoms* into the poetry. This is analogous, perhaps, to an idea advanced by Stekel (1962) that the parapathy will appear always in the dream. The parapathy, at least in the cases presented here, appeared in the early poems written by the patient. Relevant to this same point, Patterson (1973) observes in his analysis of Gestalt therapy that the dream will represent or contain in some form an unfinished or unassimilated situation. Or, as suggested by Perls (1969), the dream is, in the final analysis, an existential message. It is possible, then, to continue to relate the patient's dream and his poetry so that the poem, especially the one written early in treatment, will reveal the unwanted emotion which Perls places at the focal point in therapeutic intervention. Perls also believes the awareness of the unwanted emotion and the ability to endure this emotion may be the *conditio sine qua non* for a successful cure. This paper suggests that the unwanted emotion appears in the early poems of the patient in poetry therapy. Recovery is encouraged as these intense emotions are assimilated by means of the patient's analysis of his own poetry.

Case histories will now be presented in support of the hypothesis that the epiphany of the self may be observed in long-term treatment of patients in poetry therapy.

Case 1

This was a young college woman, age 22, suffering persistent headaches which her physician diagnosed as psychosomatic. Upon his suggestion, she sought psychological help. She was asked to write a poem on the first day of her treatment. The instructions went as follows: "Write a poem which expresses how you are feeling right now. It is not necessary that it be a good poem but that it express to the best of your ability how you are feeling." The poem she wrote was as follows:

> *I love you*
> *As I love the sea.*
> *But were I forced to choose*
> *I would choose the sea.*
> *It cannot run from me.*

According to our hypothesis, the patient had projected the parapathy into the poem. Subsequently, she was asked to pick the line of her poem which best suggested her feelings. She decided upon the line: *I would choose the sea.* This line was written out for her and she was asked to look at it, then close her eyes and say whatever came into her mind. Her dialogue is recorded as follows:

> I would choose the sea. I love to go to the ocean. I like how big it is. It's bigger than I am, bigger than everything almost. (Laughter) That's funny, isn't it? I sound like a child. "Bigger than everything." That's like when I used to have my father bring me an ice cream cone when I was little. "A really big one," I would say.

The conjecture of separation anxiety and what Horney (1942) called a morbid dependency became the tentative diagnosis in this case. After 10 hours of therapy, she was asked to write a second poem, at home this time, and to bring it in for her subsequent meeting. The second poem was as follows:

> *We cut down our own Christmas tree*
> *this year,*
> *Dragged it out of the woods, a*
> *scruffy thing,*

Not near the beauty it had seemed,
Standing there on that slope, leaning
Toward December's sun.
But I decorated it, and put a star on
top;
Stood there before that shining tree,
And some even whispered admiringly:
"I like your tree, I like your tree."

From the first poem to this second one, 10 weeks later, a movement into the transformer cycle can be seen. A tree, "a scruffy thing" is brought back from the woods and transformed into something that is admired. The patient was asked to find the line or lines she liked best. She selected the line: *Not near the beauty it had seemed.* Her response to the line of poetry was as follows:

> I'm not sure why but that line makes me think of my father. I guess it's me I'm thinking of. I wasn't a raving beauty, as you can see, I suppose, and I think my father was always disappointed. He wanted a pretty little girl he could really be proud of. (Sigh) Well, I did my best.

The following conversation took place between patient and therapist:

T: You did your best?
P: It's incredible what you can do with some paint! Make-up.
T: I wonder what it is you are feeling right now.
P: I'm feeling like I'm going to cry.
T: You're feeling sad?
P: (Crying) I just hate to do that!
T: The tree in your poem. What you called a scruffy thing.
P: What about it?
T: If you were to make that tree a person who would it be?
P: (Thoughtful) A scruffy thing. Me.
T: Let's see, what did you do with the tree, in the poem?
P: Decorated it.
T: And people admired it.
P: They said they did.
T. What do you think?
P: (Laughter) It's really amazing how you *can* decorate a scruffy old thing.

The patient discontinued therapy shortly after this session because of work conflict commitments. She was asked to write a poem on her last day. She wrote it quickly and handed it to the therapist just before leaving his office. It went as follows:

I started with a thumping sound,
Like a tire going flat on the
highway.
Fuller now, I sing a brave song to
the rain,
Thumping though, forever thumping
just the same.

Case 2

This second case was a professional man, 34, referred for poetry therapy by a clinic where he was receiving chemotherapy. His diagnosis was borderline schizophrenia. The physician in charge of his case suggested poetry therapy since the patient was filling notebooks with his own poetry. The following poem was offered by the physician as being diagnostic in itself:

Eyes find me.
Even at night they find me.
Cat eyes I think sometimes,
But there are voices, too,
Behind the eyes,
Saying I should kill myself.
One day when I pretend to
Be asleep,
I shall wait until those eyes
Are hovering just beyond my
Face,
And plunge a knife,
And watch the egg
Go running yellow;
A splash upon the whiteness
Of my shirt.

The poem itself seemed consistent with the paranoid dynamism as described by Sullivan (1956)—namely, a brooding sense of persecution. Also, there is dissociation in the last four lines as the metaphor switches, without connection, from eye to egg.

The therapist, seeing this patient for the first time, recorded the following dialogue:

T: When did you write this poem?
P: A year ago, I think. Some time back at least.
T: How do you feel about the poem?
P: I don't have any feeling about it.

T: You like it a little bit; you don't like it, what?

P: Like I said, I don't have any feelings about it at all. In a way I can't exactly remember writing it.

T: What out of the whole poem strikes you most; what line or lines, I mean?

P: "And watch the egg go running yellow," I guess, if I have to pick a line.

T: What comes to your mind as you visualize that, the egg running yellow?

P: Nothing.

T: Close your eyes and visualize the egg running yellow.

P: (Eyes closed) O.K.

T: The yellow, the running yellow. Tell me what you think it feels like.

P: Blood?

T: Is that a question?

P: Not blood, I don't think blood feels sticky.

T: The feeling is sticky?

P: Yes.

T: What does that bring to mind?

P: (Eyes open) Does this all make a whole lot of sense, what we're doing?

T: Would you close your eyes again? What comes to your mind when you touch that sticky substance, what you've called the yellow of an egg?

P: I got that! What I *call* the yellow of an egg.

T: So, what does it bring to mind?

P: Why are you playing this cat and mouse game with me? You know and I know what it brings to mind.

T: So, put it into words.

P: An ejaculation.

At this point it was apparent that, to use the language advanced by Kelly (1955), the patient needed "tightening." He was beginning to shift about quickly in his seat and blotches of red had appeared on his neck. It was suggested that he write a poem expressing his feelings at this moment. Following Kelly's construct system, writing a poem would, it is hoped, facilitate the organization of the construction system. The patient wrote the following poem:

This is a dream.
I am an auditor.
I fret in my seat
While the actors,
Behind the curtain,
Wait impatient
To be heard.

The writing of this poem did appear to "tighten" the patient. His anxiety seemed to lessen. He also seemed exhausted. The following dialogue transpired:

P: There's your poem.
T: Will you read it to me.
   (P reads the poem with what is almost disinterest.)
P: Now you want to know what's my favorite line, right?
T: How does the poem make you feel?
P: I don't feel anything.
T: Let me read it to you. You close your eyes.
P: What's the eyes closed routine?
T: So you can relax.
   (T reads the poem.)
P: Now you want my reaction, right?
T: All right.
P: Actually I did have a sort of funny sensation when you were reading it. I sort of remembered a dream. It's like the poem a little bit.
T: Could I hear the dream?
P: I dreamed this several times last year. I'm in a movie waiting for the curtain to go up or something. Then someone starts showing home movies on the curtain. (Laughter) I remember everyone in the theater became furious. We'd come to see a movie, I mean a good movie, and some ass was showing home movies.
T: Do you know what kind of movie you'd come to see?
P: No. (A covert smile)
T: What came to your mind just then?
P: Pornography.
T: Let's go back to the poem, all right?
P: You're the doctor.
T: Behind the curtain there are actors impatient to be heard.
P: Yeah.
T: What's that make you think of? Behind the curtain, actors, waiting to be heard.
P: Nothing.
T: Close your eyes. Again: behind the curtain, actors, waiting to be heard. What?
P: I had a funny impression just then.
T: Go ahead.
P: It was like the curtain was an eye lid.
T: Yes?
P: Well, the curtain is an eye lid and the voices of the actors are just inside the head. That doesn't make a whole lot of sense does it.
T: The voices of the actors are inside the head?
P: (Anxious) We have to go on with this?
T: No.

The anxiety level had increased again and it appeared the patient was approaching a state of panic. Kelly's technique of tightening was employed, the patient being encouraged to summarize what had happened to him since the time he had referred himself to the clinic for treatment. In the process of this summarization he did "tighten" and the anxiety lessened substantially. This treatment session was terminated and a subsequent session scheduled.

When he was seen the following week, he brought with him a poem which he handed over almost as if it were a ticket of admission. His emotional investment in the poem was apparent. The therapist read it once silently, then read it aloud:

> *Hidden in the branches*
> *Of an old Maple tree,*
> *I heard my Mother call*
> *My name.*
> *And for a moment I hid*
> *From her,*
> *Enjoying her moment of*
> *Despair.*
> *And then she found me,*
> *Hiding there,*
> *Her voice, a little bird:*
> *"Oh, there you are!"*

The patient had in this poem projected an identification with the child. Jung (1953) states that we meet the child-archetype in spontaneous and therapeutically induced individuation. The patient in this poem has identified himself with his infantilism. Jung suggests that under the influence of therapy this identity breaks down and a second identification appears, this time with the hero. In a treatment session 17 hours later the following poem was presented with the statement, "I wrote this over the week-end. A present for you."

> *RORSCHACH*
> *There is nothing there.*
> *Ink the exaulted have*
> *Hung their stars upon.*
> *Nothing!*
> *I could search and*
> *Find a face for you*
> *If it was worth it.*
> *"A face! See the eyes,*
> *The nose, and here, a mouth."*
> *I'll excite you and*
> *Set your pen to work:*

"I see . . . a monster!"
Ah, how pleased you are!
More?
"A monster tearing itself apart."
Your pen flies over the page.
Record my game, Dr. Star Eyes.
What I really see—
Some ink upon a page.

The trickster cycle is apparent in this poem; the patient has moved beyond the child. He is being cynical and daring, poking fun at his therapist. A change is coming over the patient. And the poem which he wrote several sessions later continued the essence of change, this time involving the sense of loss:

I am October
I am an Oak which will not
Surrender its leaves
I am the sumac which yellows
Too soon along the slopes.
I am the whisper of the first snow.
I am—October.

In this poem it appears he is moving beyond the trickster; there is the sober manifestation of facing life, a considerable advance from his first poem, which began "Eyes find me . . . "

He was asked to discuss the poem and the dialogue went as follows:

T: How do you feel about this poem?
P: Sad, I think.
T: Sad?
P: It expresses the way I feel.
T: Yes?
P: Sad in a sort of excited kind of way if that makes any sense.
T: Which line of your poem do you respond to with the greatest feeling?
P: "I am the sumac which yellows too soon . . . "
T: Why that line?
P: It's the way I feel. I'm almost 35 and it seems now like the summer went very fast if you know what I mean.
T: Yes.

In subsequent sessions, depression was the predominant emotion with this patient and the mood disorder was so intense that his physician prescribed Elevil. Employing the isoprinciple as suggested by Leedy (1969), a poem written by another depressed patient was read to this individual. Leedy observed that depressed patients often respond to poems that are sad and gloomy. This patient responded intensely to the following poem:

> *A dark house beckons to me.*
> *Ghosts escape the walls*
> *And claim my life*
> *With their melancholy song.*

"That is a poem I could have written myself," was his immediate response to the reading of the verse. The patient smiled and sat up and read the poem to himself. "That says it," he declared. "That says exactly what it is I feel. But it's funny. In that line 'Ghosts escape the walls,' it's like the walls are me. My own skin."

He said he would write a poem and bring it in the next time. "A sequel to that one," he said. And his poem was submitted the next time he appeared:

> *Rain song on the windows of my room.*
> *I am prisoner there;*
> *A song I cannot bear*
> *And yet I dread to hear it end.*

His poem was used in a free association, an attempt to gain more forward movement. The dialogue with the therapist went as follows:

T: How does your poem make you feel?
P: Very sad.
T: Go on.
P: It's not a very good poem.
T: What line do you especially like?
P: "A song I cannot bear."
T: What does that bring to your mind: "A song I cannot bear."
P: (Laughter)
T: What?
P: You won't believe what came to my mind.
T: Go ahead.
P: Melancholy Baby. Some guy playing at a piano bar played it last summer. I'd never heard it before.
T: Melancholy Baby.
P: Yeah.

The patient brought the following poem into his therapy session nearly a month later.

In an old house
Where I was born
I found a picture
Which I hardly recognized.
"So that is you," my father said.
I looked away in pain.

He became very emotional upon reading this poem and cried intensely, apologizing profusely, and all the while accusing himself of being a child. It was obvious that some wisdom (the twins) was emerging. He was beginning to experience the insight judged in this case to be necessary for the further epiphany of his self. The dialogue with the therapist went as follows:

T: That poem upsets you.
P: You might say that.
T: What is it—?
P: It's dumb, getting upset over something you yourself wrote.
T: What in the poem upsets you?
P: " 'So that is you,' my father said."
T: That line?
P: Yes.
T: Why?
P: There is something sad about it.
T: Imagine the scene in the poem. Your father and you looking at the picture.
P: It's hard to do.
T: Try. What do you see, the picture?
P: It's a child.
T: Close your eyes and relax. Get as relaxed as you possibly can.
P: O.K.
T: Let's look at the picture again, you and I. What do you see?
P: A tree.
T: Anything else?
P: A man, in the distance.
T: Which direction is he facing?
P: Straight out, sort of this way.
T: Who does he look like?
P: (Laughter) You, I think.
T: Look a little closer.
P: Me, a little bit.

Shortly after this, the patient discontinued therapy. He did not write any more poems, claiming lack of time and inspiration. He reported a dream, however, which he said made him feel good. And the dream he said was like the poem he would have written, time and energy permitting. His dream was as follows:

> I am standing underneath an apple tree in the bright sun. I look up and see that the tree is really loaded with apples, the brightest, healthiest apples I had ever seen. I felt really happy in the dream.

Case 3

This patient was a 23-year-old college senior, a black girl with an IQ measurement of 138 on the Wechsler Bellevue. Her symptom was as follows: "I feel like I am going to explode." Her physician had recommended that she seek some kind of psychotherapy, her moderately high blood pressure being possibly due to undeflected rage. Her first poem was written at home and brought into the third session of therapy.

> *TO A LOST DOG*
> *Did they cast you out?*
> *Tire of you like some used up toy?*
> *You sit now, your eyes opaque,*
> *Trembling against the street lamp,*
> *Waiting for a familiar hand*
> *To snap your collar chain again*
> *And lead you home.*
>
> *But they are gone now,*
> *Those who called you* pet
> *And scratched your ears,*
> *And sometimes let you crawl*
> *In bed with them.*
> *Halfway around the world,*
> *Gone—*
> *And you'll forget in time.*

This poem was analyzed with the patient as follows:

T: What is the main idea of the poem?
P: A lost dog.
T: How has he come to be lost?
P: His people went on vacation and they just dumped him out so they wouldn't have the problem of a kennel or anything.
T: Why do you think you wrote this poem?
P: You asked me to write a poem.
T: Why do you think you wrote this particular poem?

P: I feel for lost dogs. (Laughter) I specialize in feeling for lost dogs.
T: Do you know the emotion yourself?
P: Doesn't everyone?
T: You mean you know the emotion?
P: Sure. I think everyone does.

The patient returned to the next session very depressed and almost unwilling to talk. To the request that she write a poem which expressed her feelings, she wrote:

In the middle of the street,
I see that the sun has
Cast the world half in shadow.
A tree, bright on one side,
Shadow on the other.

The writing of the poem seemed to have the effect of abreaction. She began to respond to the therapist and the following dialogue ensued:

T: What is the theme of this poem?
P: Sort of half and half.
T: What does that mean?
P: I don't know exactly, half light half dark, I guess.
T: What does that statement bring to mind?
P: Me.
T: You?
P: Half light half dark. Half black half white. My father's French.
T: I see. (A long silence)
     How does the poem make you feel? (Therapist reads it.) What is your feeling as you hear the poem?
P: No feeling.

In a subsequent session the patient declined to write a poem but did report a dream:

I dreamed that I was watching a Catholic school from across the street. I heard a fire alarm and saw nuns coming outside in a hurry. That's the dream.

She expressed little feeling in recounting the dream and seemed almost to deny it had anything to do with her. The following dialogue took place.

T: You were watching in the dream?
P: Yes.
T: And you saw—

P: Nuns.

T: What was their emotion?

P: They were frightened—terror-stricken actually.

T: So the emotion is terror.

P: In the dream, yes, terror.

T: What were the nuns wearing?
     (A lengthy pause)

P: Black.

T: Could you see their faces?

P: Yes.

T: Describe.

P: (With controlled sarcasm) Little round white faces.

T: Black on the outside—

P: White on the inside.

T: What does that make you think of? (A long hesitation)
     Black on the outside, white on the inside.

P: It's me again.

T: How is it you again?

P: You know what I've been considering? Going to live in Los Angeles.
     People say I could pass for white in Los Angeles; marry a white guy.

T: I see.

P: I'm suddenly very angry with you, Doctor.

T: Angry with me—
     (The patient abruptly left the office.)

She did not come for her appointment the following week. She called later and requested another appointment. This was arranged and she arrived on time but would not say one word. She sat for 50 minutes, not looking at the therapist and not responding once to his efforts to begin their session. At the end of the scheduled period, the therapist said, "Our time is up," and the patient got up and walked quickly out of the room, stopping in the outer office to make an appointment for the following week. When she returned the following week, she brought this poem:

> Like two sandpipers we played
> On the beach,
> Running in and out
> With the waves,
> Playing with love
> Until the sun, bleeding,
> Lay at the horizon.

The following dialogue between patient and therapist took place:

T: Why do you think you wrote this poem?

P: This is poetry therapy so I wrote a poem. Like you want me to do.

T: I wonder why about sandpipers?

P: I saw a movie called *The Sandpiper*.

T: I see. What would you say your poem is about?

p: I don't know. Love?

T: What are the sandpipers doing?

P: Playing with the waves.

T: Playing.

P: Yes.

T: What does the word playing bring to your mind?

P: When I was little.

At this point, we can see the projection of the child. The patient has reached the first step in the epiphany of a self. The next several poems she wrote dealt with the theme of the child again. For her 27th therapy session, she brought in the following poem, which she handed over like a gift, not the arrogant expectation of rejection which had in some way characterized her earlier reactions.

Have you noticed that the sun doesn't shine any more?
It's up there in the sky, but it doesn't shine any more.
It just sits there, a little bit white,
Moving, crossing the sky, hot even—but it doesn't shine
Any more.

I remember when I was little and the sun would shine
In the morning, coming up over the top of
Grandpap's old house;
Shine, in that way it doesn't any more.

I wonder why it is there the sun doesn't shine any more.
Round object up there, radiance all gone,
Crossing toward the hills, hot, causing the earth
To crack like a checker board.
But it doesn't shine.

It is curious, don't you think, a sun that doesn't shine?
Is it enough to have a sun that shoulders its way
Up in the morning and ploughs across the sky,
Settling at night into a purple wash beyond the river?
Is it enough?

Mother, why doesn't the sun shine any more?

The patient seemed especially sad as the poem was read, but the emotion was not depression. She readily talked about the poem:

T: What have you said in this poem?
P: The sun doesn't shine any more. I got that message across.
T: What *is* the message?
P: I don't know.
T: Let's see if we can figure it out.
P: I had one thought.
T: Yes.
P: It relates to what we talked about before. Me being black.
T: How is that?
P: Well, I think in the poem I'm sort of coming to terms with being black.
T: Can you explain this to me?
P: I can't explain it, it's just something I think.

The epiphany of the self continued to be reflected in the poetry of this patient. Subsequent to a trip to New York, she wrote the following poem about the Verrazano Bridge:

Verrazano, stretched from here to there,
Holding enormous weight—precious weight—
Without the slightest threat of falling to the sea.
Verrazano, are you what you seem to be?

Here the patient examines her new self-concept, asking the question "Am I what I seem to be?" She is expressing an identification with the bridge which is an element of the transformer part of self. A bridge goes from here to there, just as the growing (transforming) self goes from here to there.

Her next poem, written during the session, was a continuing manifestation of the growing self:

I want to be a bird;
To fly over the top of things.
To reach toward the sun
And look back at all that lies below—
In perspective now.

During this same session, she reported a dream that seemed to go on all night long. It was an exhausting dream, which ended at last with a sense of relief. The dream is reported below:

I go up to a ticket counter and try to get a ticket on a big airplane. I can see it out on the field, the biggest airplane I've ever seen. The clerk behind the desk fusses around and doesn't ever seem to get down to the business of getting me a ticket. I go over to another airline window and ask for a ticket there. I can see this airplane outside on the runway. And the girl behind the counter gives me my ticket. I run outside and someone says "You don't have to run; it'll wait for you." Just as I board I see the other plane, the big one and for just a second the sun seems to flash off the aluminum skin or whatever. Then I go inside the smaller plane and I notice how bright and cheerful it is inside and I tell the hostess "This looks like my living room."

The patient was graduating in May, and there were only two more sessions before she left the university. She wrote one more poem. The elements of the twins appears, the emergence of wisdom in the self system.

Last summer I drove across
The desert in my old car.
We labored, that machine and I.
And when we got across I fed
Both it and I the water
That we needed to survive.
It guzzled, took its fill at once;
While I—lest I should get sick—
Drank with measure,
Waiting for the sense of being filled.

The patient reported a dream during her last session before graduation. The dream went as follows:

I was standing at the top of the stairs in an old house where we used to live. I felt something coming right through my skin and I grabbed it. It was a white doll, made of alabaster, and white as chalk. I threw it down the steps and saw it break up into little pieces. And I heard my father crying off somewhere in the house.

The therapist asked her. "Do you think you need to discuss what you're saying in this dream?" Her response was: "I don't think it needs translation." The therapist agreed and her case was ended several sessions later.

Concluding Remarks

This paper has attempted to find empirical support for the Jungian hypothesis that the self emerges in hierarchy—the child being the first manifestation, followed by the hero, the immediate prototype of the self. The investigation of the poems of three patients suggests that the first projection may be the parapathy itself; the individual writes about his preoccupation, the illness. When the child archetype first appears in the poetry of the patient, this may be taken as evidence of movement in therapy. And when the elements of the hero appear, as differentiated by Radin (trickster, transformer, Red Horn, twins), further development in the epiphany of self is manifest.

One additional construct became apparent in the study of these three case histories: the poems written in therapy may reflect the same unconscious process as that found in the dreams of patients. Jung (1968) believed that dreams illuminated the patient's situation in a way that could be beneficial to health. He felt that dreams awakened dormant unconscious elements in relationships.

Perhaps the poetry of a patient can do this same thing. In that case, poetry therapy would be a valuable adjunct to analytical therapy. Gutheil (1951) in his dream analysis sometimes employed this technique. In discussing one patient whose "dreamwork" led into the recall of a poem, Stekel (1962) observed that the poem, better than any report, illustrated the patient's infantilism. In this case, the poem, stimulated by the dream, had revealed in the patient a strong family fixation which was interfering with her heterosexual adjustment. Freud pointed out how individuals resist dream-thoughts to penetrating their consciousness. Again, poetry therapy may be an important adjunct when access to the unconscious appears to be blocked.

References

Freud, Sigmund. *The interpretation of dreams*. New York: Science Editions, 1961.

Gutheil, Emil. *The handbook of dream analysis*. New York: Grove Press, 1951.

Horney, Karen. *Self-analysis*. New York: Norton, 1942.

Jung, C. G. *Psyche and symbol*. New York: Doubleday, 1953.

Jung, C. G. *Two essays on analytical psychology*. New York: Meridian Books, 1956.

Jung, C. G. "The psychotherapeutic value of dreams." In *The structure and dynamics of the psyche*. Princeton, N.J.: Princeton University Press, 1968. Pp. 288-296.

Kelly, G. A. *The psychology of personal constructs*. Vol. 1. *A theory of personality*. Vol. 2. *Clinical diagnosis and psychotherapy*. New York: Norton, 1955.

Leedy, J. J. (Ed.) *Poetry therapy*. Philadelphia: Lippincott, 1969.

Patterson, C. H. *Theories of Counseling and psychotherapy*. New York: Harper & Row, 1973.

Perls, F. S. *Ego hunger and aggression*. New York: Random House, 1961.

Perls, F. S. *Gestalt therapy verbatim*. Moab, Utah: Real People Press, 1969.

Radin, Paul. *Hero cycles of the Winnebago*. Bloomington: Indiana University, 1948.

Stekel, Wilhelm. *The interpretation of dreams*. New York: Grosset & Dunlap, 1962.

Sullivan, Harry Stack. *The collected works of Harry Stack Sullivan*. New York: Norton, 1956.

CHAPTER 4

Parsing Concepts: A Discovery Technique for Poetry Therapy *

Robert N. Ross

A Simple Demonstration

I gave a class of poetry students a poem by Emily Dickinson with the instructions that they were "to take the poem apart" into what seemed to them isolated wholes. I called the pieces "conceptual units" for convenience, and by that I meant they were recognizable integers whose meaning would be lost if they were further divided. Each student was to list these conceptual units as he found them for himself and then number them in the order they appear in the poem. I called this "parsing the poem" because it is an operation done on the meanings of the text similar to the operations of parsing syntax. In both cases a whole unit is resolved into its component parts; then, by labeling the parts, it is shown how they relate to each other in the whole.

Students found these parses easy to do and also instructive because it made them focus their attention on relationships in the text they never suspected. A typical parse of the Dickinson poem looks like this.

The poem:

> There is a solitude of space
> A solitude of sea
> A solitude of death, but these
> Society shall be
> Compared with that profounder site
> That polar privacy

*Research for this paper was funded in part by a grant from The National Council of Teachers of English and an Andrew Mellon Post-Doctoral Fellowship from the University of Pittsburgh.

A soul admitted to itself—
Finite infinity. *

The parse of the poem:
1. There is a solitude of space
2. A solitude of sea
3. A solitude of death
4. but these
5. Society shall be compared with
6. that profounder site
7. That polar privacy
8. A soul admitted to itself
9. Finite infinity

I found very little variation in these parses. Students tended to find and list the same or very similar constituents of meaning in the poem.

The second part of this experiment was for each student to recombine the items of the parse in a way that reconstituted his own understanding of the poem. I call it "construing." The instructions were to connect with lines the items of content parsed out of the poem in the first exercise. The lines drawn between the items are to show that they are somehow connected, but I left the kind of connection represented by the line completely unspecified. As long as items of the parse were associated in thinking, they could be joined by a line in the diagram. In this exercise I found a bit less agreement, but it was still considerable. Figure 4-1 is a typical diagram.

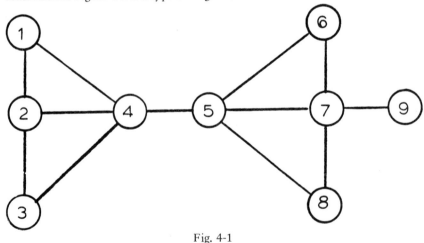

Fig. 4-1

*From Poems by EMILY DICKINSON. Edited by Martha Dickinson Bianchi and Alfred Leete Hampson. Copyright 1914, 1942 by Martha Dickinson Bianchi and reprinted by permission of Little, Brown and Co.

The structure we see in networks of parsed items as shown in Fig. 4-1 corresponds quite closely with the structure of meanings people find in the poem. My conclusion was that people tend to agree about the ways in which pieces of content can be parsed out of the whole context of a poem and about the ways they perceive meaningful relationships among these pieces of content. There was, for example, almost complete consensus in identifying the items of the parse and general, if not unanimous, agreement on how the pieces of the parse fit together. However, when I asked those people who had connected items of their parses to say more about the connections they showed in their diagrams, all consensus disintegrated. Apparently consensus obtains at only the most superficial levels of understanding.

One reason for the lack of consensus here is that we are all unaccustomed to thinking about thinking. Inventing categories for thought is the problem of logic, and students are naturally stymied when asked to so invent. To avoid this difficulty, I provided students with a list of categories (such as equivalence, conjunction, disjunction, negation, agent of action, patient, object, etc.) drawn from symbolic logic, grammar, and rhetoric. The central problem was to choose one or more labels from the list that described a particular connection shown in the diagram. I was delighted to find that students now had no difficulty labeling the connections, but I was chagrined to find that consensus was still no better. Students could label connections, but they could not agree on what might be an appropriate label. I then concluded that we agree about the meanings of the text only at the most superficial levels. For example, the initial parse, which takes the text apart into its so-called conceptual units, follows the syntax fairly closely. But since we learn syntax as we learn our language, it is no wonder that when one is called upon to perform a syntactic act, as in parsing a poem, he can do it with ease and pretty much as everyone else does.

We are not taught, however, to put meanings together. Symbolic logic formalizes some aspects of this process; but even then, symbolic logic is far too limiting and formal to do much good in representing the ways in which our minds work upon the material of our experience. So when it comes to parsing the text of a poem and putting the parts of the text back together again, we are thrown upon our own semantic resources. We have few, if any, conventional models to follow.

But this loose construction we put on poems is precisely their virtue for poetry therapy because not all of us assemble bits of meaning in the same way. No matter how much we may agree on what might be the conceptual units, each of us fits the pieces together according to his own lights. This gets at the intuition lying at the heart of poetry therapy—namely that what people say about a poem says a lot about them as people.

Still there is a serious theoretical problem. "As far as I am aware," wrote George A. Miller, "no objective methods for the direct appraisal of *contents* have been devised, either by linguists or psychologists" (p. 569, 1971). This statement is both true and discouraging, for such methods are the very tool that poetry therapists need. Therapists are called upon to make normative judgments about the emotions and understandings below the surface of a poem written by a client or underlying the client's comments about another poem. Yet we lack the formal, or even informal, semantic theory for making such connections of word and thought. Given our present understanding of the psychology of language, perhaps we should try a different approach, stressing the combination possibilities of conceptual units within the poem instead of the meaning of individual words. Let us look at how people arrange content within a poem to satisfy their specific needs. This selection and combining of units to form meaningful wholes is what I called "parsing" and "construing" (the conceptual parse) in my discussion of the Dickinson poem.

What I propose, therefore, is a method that in effect will permit an analysis of the parts without losing a sense of the whole. To accomplish this purpose, I shall employ the science of combinations formalized as graph theory. We can thus describe the relations of concepts in interlocking networks and also have a formalism that is rich enough to give us new orders of information from the words of the text and loose enough to keep us from being dominated by it. By having patients make such graphs of poems, we shall have a discovery technique for analyzing their conceptual as well as their verbal structure.

But before I present the conceptual parse formally and apply it to therapeutic situations, I must say a few things about language.

Language and Behavior

Language, like behavior, is patterned, meaningful, and deliberate. These are terms that I associate with the more strictly linguistic notions of syntax, semantics, and pragmatics. Syntax is descriptive. It describes the systematic ways in which words combine with each other to form phrases and clauses and then how these combine to form sentences. Selection, combination, and arrangement of units called "syntagms" are its field of inquiry. And because syntagms are formed by the combination of one unit with another, the description is a linear one in which strings of connections adequately describe the sets of interactions between the units.

Semantics, on the other hand, is not linear. If we can call syntax *descriptive*, we can call semantics *ascriptive*. Semantics is the study of how we ascribe meanings systematically to the structures and patterns described by syntax. Semantics also presupposes fields of meaning interacting among the words, thoughts, and behavior of people. Finally, pragmatics is neither a linear nor a field phenomenon. Since it is what people do to their worlds by means of their language, the study of pragmatics is essentially a cybernetic study, for the relations of language and action are inextricably bound up with one another. One feeds back on the other and defines it.

When we discuss poems written by patients, we are dealing with all three kinds of organization: the linear sequence of syntagms, the field relations of meanings within that mental intermediary between perception and conception (*Zwischenswelt*), and the cybernetic relations of meanings and intentions. Needless to say, in analyzing the materials used in poetry therapy, we need the most sophisticated models of language and thought available to identify the mental process revealed by the verbal structure.

For this very reason, behaviorist models of language are too reductionist. In the behaviorist's zeal for determining quantifiable variables, he too often cuts the stream of behavior into pieces too fine to be interesting or useful. The connections that make them meaningful are lost. The problem is that language can be arbitrarily segmented into all sorts of fragmentary *-emes* (phoneme, morpheme, lexeme, sememe, etc.), but our conception of the world cannot.

What has all this to do with therapy in general and poetry therapy in particular? One of the chief characteristics of poetic symbol and metaphor is that a complex set of relations is summed up as a single whole. This is called "condensation" and it holds in psychoanalytic thought as it does in the theory of poetry. The singular opportunity afforded by these graphs is that it allows us to unravel some of the lines contributing to the condensed figure of the symbol. The reason for this is that the symbol does not exist in a vacuum.

Consequently, we can trace the lines connecting the symbol to the rest of the context. If we do this, even quite mechanically by tracing lines of the graphs, we begin to see all the ligatures tying the particular symbol into the structure of the whole content. This, then, becomes a comment, an exegesis of the symbol itself; for the connecting lines holding the particular symbol to the context of the whole are the very aspects of the symbol that are meaningful. We can expand the symbol by attending to the relations of the graph.

We should distinguish, however, between two kinds of symbols, both of which depend upon their context for their meaning. Reference symbols, like the sink tap, symbolize water because they suggest it. We learn from our experience that we can get water from a mechanical contrivance. Of far greater interest, if we want to know how people cut up the cognitive mass of their world, are the condensation symbols. These are emotionally charged metaphors and other symbols for which we substitute more manageable materials (words and other symbols) for the highly charged and problematic materials of life. We do this all the time, of course, but there are times when the symbols of condensation are especially noteworthy.

For instance, if we are interested in the poems written by an emotionally disturbed person, we should pay strict attention to these condensation symbols since, as we have said, they are substitutions. In the language behavior itself, in the attitudes toward the symbols, in the symbolic actions expressed by them, we can see the actions the person would have done but for the subterfuge of the symbol. In part, the symbol is the symptom; it can be studied in the same way that we study other symptoms for its connections with the pathology.

Discovering the Structure of Content: The Conceptual Parse

The conceptual parse is a method by which poems can be reduced to graphs and the graphs analyzed by various mathematical techniques (Ross, 1974). This gives us a fairly rigorous method for describing and analyzing the structure of content. By this I mean (1) that content can be decomposed to its constituent items; (2) that the text we study comprises a set of ordered relations among these items of content; (3) that this set of ordered relations can be translated to a symbolic system which is simpler than the text itself; (4) that such a system is simpler because it attends primarily to the relations between items of content and not particularly to their connotative complexities; and (5) that we can translate the simpler system back into the content of the poem. If we did not mind the sheer mechanical difficulties of manipulating pieces of the text itself, we could perform every operation on it that we do on its symbolic representation as a graph.

Sets of relations like these are best shown by the conventional presentation of a graph. I am using the term "graph" in a special way—I mean by it any of three different but related sets of figures. One kind of graph is simply a set of points connected by lines to indicate that these points (and whatever they stand for) are logically related. Figure 4-2 shows an example of such a graph. A second kind of graph is a set of points connected by arrows to show that one can get from one point to another by following the directions of the arrows and that some routes through the graph are prohibited because the arrows point in the wrong direction. Figure 4-3 shows such a graph. The graph shown in Fig. 4-2 is a

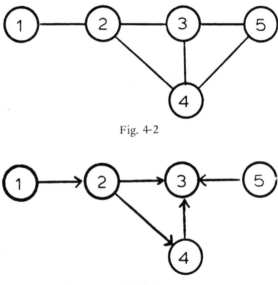

Fig. 4-2

Fig. 4-3

network; the graph shown in Fig. 4-3 is a directed graph, or *digraph*. Networks are static while digraphs are dynamic. Networks, naturally, do not show processes; but they do show enduring relations in the way that maps show geographic relations. Digraphs, on the other hand, show the time-oriented relations of process.

A third kind of graph useful to us is the one in which the connections between the points are given some kind of functional label. An example of one such labeled graph is given in Fig. 4-4. The pluses and minuses labeling the connections could be used to indicate whether the people (symbolized by the numbered nodes) who speak to each other (symbolized by the directions of the arrows) speak in friendship (+) or anger (-).

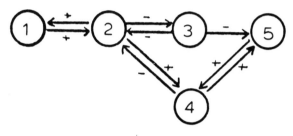

Fig. 4-4

Eventually we shall develop an extensive set of labels with which to describe the content of poems, but first I should like to present an idealized application of these graph concepts to show their special powers. If it is granted that we can translate texts into network graphs such as these, and that a text can stand as the realization of such a graph, then we have a rich formalism for discussing conceptual structures.

The beauty of this graphic method is that it avoids words where it should avoid them and allows us to reintroduce them where we want to. When we do the analytic work (take the formal structures apart), we should be bound by the rules of structures, not by the conventions of content. We need to operate upon widely diverse organizations of content as if they were, indeed, all realizations of an underlying idea discovered in their common structure. Thus, in addition to the simple economy of this graphic representation, there is a compelling logical reason for the graphs. They can do something that words simply cannot do: describe part-whole relations directly by showing how parts of the structure go together to make up the structure of the whole.

A second benefit of this graphic method is that it allows a systematic set of operational definitions. We have been using notions of structure for a long time with no clear vocabulary for discussing the constituent relations. Now, using the terminology of graph theory, and a simple terminology at that, we can make precise statements of the kinds of relations existing between parts and wholes. And, since graph theory is general enough to cover many different sorts of structure, the vocabulary we draw from graph theory is practically universal in application. This universality of our working vocabulary is a great advance. For the first time, we have a method for comparing structures with reference to their many different possibilities.

When we want to analyze particular parts of the text in relation to the structure of the whole, we must shift our focus from the whole to the part. When we do this, the part usurps the role once played by the whole. In some strange way it becomes a whole of its own, and this new-found autonomy prevents our reassociating it with the text from which it was drawn. For example, in the Dickinson poem, "Finite infinity" has different meanings; but those we choose to combine with the meanings of "A soul admitted to itself" depend completely upon our understanding of the whole poem. Nonetheless, when we begin to probe the possible meanings of "Finite infinity," we easily forget the poem from which it comes.

A second advantage in therapy of having a method for combinations is that when we begin to study a poem we have a basis for comparing apparently similar, as well as dissimilar, structures. We can do this combining by inspection, comparing one graph with another, but we can also make the comparisons mathematically. Two graphs with the same number of points connected in the same ways by the same number of lines are identical. Two graphs connected by few or no lines in common are thereby dissimilar. But they are also related because they deal with the same number of points corresponding to the same conceptual units. Obviously, there are many intermediate stages between the two graphs. There is in fact an algorithm for computing the relative similarity/dissimilarity of any two such graphs (Ross, 1973). Thus, we can compare and contrast patterns of decision about poems by asking different people to make graphs of the same poem. Similarities and dissimilarities in the patterns of the graphs will reflect similar patterns in the decision-making processes of the people drawing the graphs. Words do not allow us this kind of precision. Numbers do.

Numbers and texts have not gotten along well together in the past. But the graphs (as I shall show in the next few paragraphs) yield us an unusual kind of number. These numbers, unlike those used in the descriptions we associate with the physical sciences, are quite legitimately expressive of what we might call verbal-conceptual relations. They are numbers capable of showing relation but nothing else. They do not in any way show relative magnitudes as the numbers 50 and 100 do when measuring quantities such as tons.

Our conventional notion of number (professional mathematicians aside) is that of a straight line arbitrarily cut into equal unit lengths. But, as I have said, conceptual structures do not fall into such scalar relations. Some measures do (for example, weight, length, height, etc.), but conceptual structures are not only linear in this way, they are also fields and cybernetic systems, as we have seen. And so we need a metric structure (if there is such a thing) in which there may be numbers, but the numbers do not really correspond to arbitrary markers along a number line like the one shown in Fig. 4-5. What we need is a number system of relations in which the relations themselves define the meaning of the numbers.

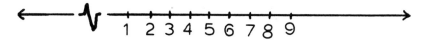

Fig. 4-5

There is such a system, and it is not a very complicated one. Take that number line and make the distances between the points irrelevant. The only determinants of number then are:

1)   that the line is somehow divided by points and
2)   that the points exist on the line in a particular order.

This new sort of number line is shown in Fig. 4-6. This frees us from some very limiting constraints. In the scalar number systems, we cannot have a right triangle like the one shown in Fig. 4-7. As Euclid demonstrated for his geometry, in a right triangle the sum of the squares of the two sides equals the square of the hypotenuse. Not even in the fancy "spaces" of other geometries can such a triangle exist. In the number system, I propose to handle the mathematics of relations so that we can easily have such a triangle. This is our freedom and the special power of this peculiar sort of quantifying. For example, let the triangle shown in Fig. 4-7 represent the number of stops a bus makes in driving the course mapped by the triangle. The lines of the triangle are streets; the numbers are the number of stops into which each street is divided. We now have a conceptual map of the bus route.

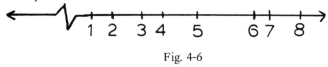

Fig. 4-6

This is not a new geometry at all, actually. The science of topology, which has been steadily developing since its inception in the 19th century, is the science of relations, the properties of geometric configurations, invariant despite the various distortions of the geometric figure. That invariance is important. As far as students of topology are concerned, the three graphs shown in Fig. 4-8 are all the same topological figure. Despite the apparent distortions of the figure on the page, they are all the same. They are invariant because if we ask which point connects with which other points, we get the same answer in each case. That is,

POINT	CONNECTS WITH
(1)	(2) and (4)
(2)	(1) and (3)
(3)	(2) and (4)
(4)	(3) and (1)

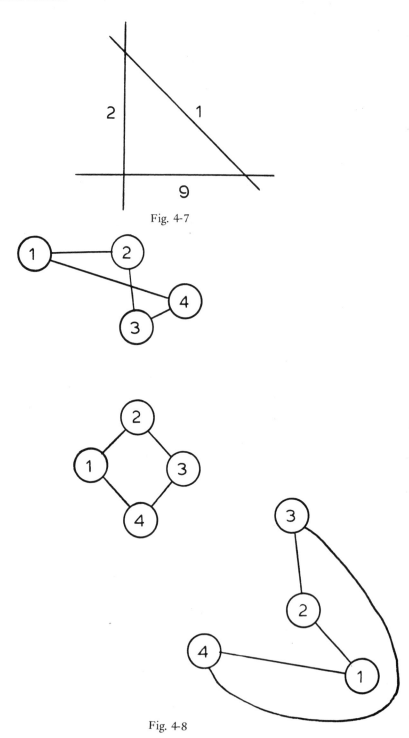

Fig. 4-7

Fig. 4-8

If all these conditions hold true in different geometric configurations, regardless of how the figure looks as we draw it on the page, they are all topologically identical.

What this means in terms of our discussion of conceptual structures is that we can map them as we never could before. The question of paraphrase, for instance, sheds light on what I mean. In some way, despite the apparent differences in how the following sentences look, they all mean roughly the same thing:

a. John closed the door.
b. The door was closed by John.
c. John saw to it that the door was no longer open.
d. It's John's fault that we could not go out that way.

In many ways these sentences mean different things, but I am not especially interested in the difference now. I want to inquire into the similarities. If the question we ask deals with the status of the door, then they are all very similar sentences.

Finally, having a topological presentation of essentially conceptual relations gives us the mathematical powers I mentioned earlier. Topology has developed definitions of such abstract qualities as the shapes of geometric figures, the vulnerability of figures to distortion and disruption, the diameter, and so forth. That means that we now have a way of formally describing the relations within texts that give the texts their meaning. But we have already seen that different people construct different meanings out of the same materials furnished by the text. And here is where the method pays off for poetry therapy. It is the closest thing we have to mind reading, for the characteristic ways of putting the text together can be described by mapping the poems in this way. And the characteristic mappings correspond very well with the characteristic patterns of thought.

No discussion of language is as ironclad as it pretends to be. But, we should be convinced enough of the sufficiency of this graph-theoretic method for analyzing the connectedness of concepts within texts to prompt us to look beyond the obvious limitations and reservations imposed by our present understanding of language and thought. We should be looking toward new methods for investigating the old questions that have so far proved intractable.

A Demonstration of the Conceptual Parse

I shall show my own parse and graph of the Dickinson poem cited earlier to show what information we can get from the method. I parsed the poem as follows:

1. There is a solitude
2. of space
3. of sea

4.   of death
5.   but these/Society shall be
6.   compared with
7.   that profounder site
8.   that polar privacy
9.   A soul admitted to itself
10.   Finite infinity.

Before showing my graph, perhaps it would be helpful if I told my paraphrase of the poem:

> There are three kinds of solitude (space, sea, and death); these three solitudes will seem as congenial as society itself when compared with the inwardness of the soul, of which there are two expressions (profounder site and polar privacy) and a kind of apposite (finite infinity).

My graph, a network of the static relations obtaining among these bits of content, is shown in Fig. 4-9.

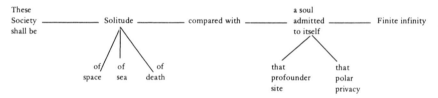

Fig. 4-9

What do we learn from it? We see that the text is built of two equivalences held together by a comparison. In particular, the equivalence of points 5 and 1 balances the equivalence of 9 and 10. But the first equivalent pair is paradoxical (that Solitude should be Society) and depends upon the absolute equivalence of the second pair (the "Finite infinity" of "A soul admitted to itself"). The graph shown in Fig. 4-10 expresses this logical structure of the poem. The point of the

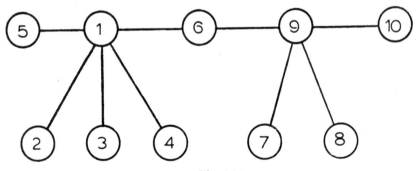

Fig. 4-10

poem is that such spatiotemporal isolations as those of space, sea, and even death are nothing compared with the absolute isolation of the individual living within his own soul.

We can perhaps see why Emily Dickinson inverted the order in which she presented some parts of the content. In effect, she has worked a transformation of the conceptual structure of the poem, moving the point or logical subject of the poem from its conventional initial position to another position embedded deeper in the poem. Point 5, which should appear first in the logical structure of the argument, is delayed. The same can be said of point 9. Like 5, it too is delayed: in the straightforward presentation of the content, it should have followed 6. The graph is a formal method for representing these purposeful transformations of the content.

We have identified the formal operations; but what do they mean? Among many other things, the delaying of points 5 and 9, moving them from their most straightforward logical positions, raises other points of the poem to prominence. Specifically, 1, 7, and 8. A text, after all, is a network of intimate relations. Moving one part of the network must affect all the other points. In this case, the notions of "Solitude," "profounder site," and "polar privacy" are raised to prominence by the lowering of "Society" and "A soul admitted to itself."

If we were studying a poem written by a client, this sort of information would be useful indeed. We would gain a powerful insight into the dynamics of how that client actively organized his thinking and feeling.

We may also wish to treat these relations purely as relations, dispensing for the moment with the bits of text. We can treat this map as a contentless graph of connected points. We do this, of course, for the sake of convenience. It is easier to manipulate the graph's numbered relations than it is to manipulate the graph's pieces of the text. After analyzing the connections within the contentless graph, we can again introduce the content and see what the purely mathematical and formal analyses have added to our understanding of the content. The graph of numbered relations (that is, with the content removed) is shown in Fig. 4-10. Shown this way, we can easily see the nice symmetry with which Emily Dickinson ordered the contents of the poem. Node 5 neatly balances its opposite, node 10. Society is the great foil for "Finite infinity." Solitude, the apparent isolation, has hanging from it three dependent qualifiers; soul, the true isolation, has two dependent qualifiers hanging from it. And, finally, we see that the poem structures the content in such a way that one end is the mirror image of the other. If we take node 6 as the central point, we see that nodes 1 and 9 are functionally identical; also 5 and 10 are functionally identical. Now we can "put the content in motion," as it were, by giving simple labels to the connections in the graph. The labels correspond roughly to the function relating the points connected. As shown in Fig. 4-11, I shall use three functions only: *equivalence* (shown by the double two-headed arrow), *governor-dependent* relation (shown by the single-headed arrow pointing from the governor to the dependent), and the *object* relation (shown by the double

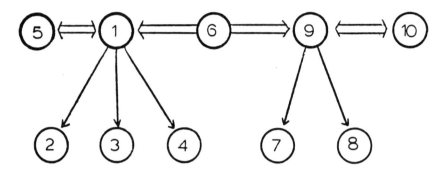

Fig. 4-11

single-headed arrow pointing toward the object). Now, instead of having a static network, we have a digraph.

We can imagine that the graph shown in Fig. 4-10 is a map of the poem. In reading the poem, we trace the paths marked by the arrows. (This is a map of *my* reading only. Other people would blaze a different trail through the poem.) But, given my reading and its paraphrase, we discover striking details of structure. We have already mentioned the symmetry of the poem. Another is the centrality of node 6, not only to the structure (as shown in the static network diagram) but to the process (as shown by the digraph). If the reading (that is, understanding process) does not begin with node 6, it is virtually impossible to reach all the nodes of the graph. In terms of reading and understanding the poem, if the reading does not begin with the comparison, it is impossible to hold together all the bits of content which comprise the poem.

With this, we are almost in a position to compare different readings of the poem by different subjects.

Let us return to the graph of the Dickinson poem shown in Fig. 4-1 and compare it with the graph shown in Fig. 4-10. What are the differences and how can we account for them?

The graph in Fig. 4-10 is more ordered. It is less homogeneous. By that I mean, there are fewer lines connecting the pieces of content and each of them serves its purpose. The graph in Fig. 4-1, on the other hand, has everything connected with everything. This, I would say, betrays the reader's confused and undifferentiated understanding of the poem.

Furthermore, the graph shown in Fig. 4-10 leads to more insights into the structure of content than does the graph shown in Fig. 4-1. The mirror-image and the stark symmetry are not so clear in the earlier graph, nor are the dependencies (shown in Fig. 4-11). And this is yet another way of expressing the confusion apparent in that reader's graph. Not only are there too many lines connecting everything with everything, but there is clearly no subordination of some content to other content. It all exists on the same plane. And yet, the dependency of examples ("space," "sea," "death," "profounder site," "polar privacy") upon the things they exemplify ("Solitude"; "A soul admitted to itself") is the essential point of the poem.

Can we now account for the differences we see between the graph shown in Fig. 4-1 and the one shown in Fig. 4-10? If we can, then we have a useful tool for representing graphically the different constructions we put on poems. Structure itself becomes apparent.

The answer is simple. The difference between the graphs can be traced to a misconception. The graph shown in Fig. 4-1 parses the lines "but these/Society shall be/Compared with that profounder site . . . " as follows: "but these// Society shall be compared with//that profounder site." The graph shown in Fig. 4-10 is drawn from a parse of the same lines, which goes: "but these Society shall be//compared with//that profounder site." Differences in the parse reveal individual differences in structuring the content, and these formal differences reveal important differences in people's understanding the poem.

Finally, this formal method of graphing a reader's understanding of a poem suggests a therapeutic procedure. When we have identified where in the text an idiosyncratic reading pathologically distorts meaning, we can work on it. In poetry therapy, workers do not usually deal with mere verbal misconceptions. In many ways my example is too simple. But when we have a full index of labels for these connections holding conceptions together, we shall be able to make more sophisticated analyses of how people construe meanings for themselves.

References

Miller, G. A. "Empirical methods in the study of semantics." In D. D. Steinberg & L. A. Jakobovitz (Eds.), *Semantics: An interdisciplinary reader in philosophy, linguistics and psychology*. Cambridge, Mass.: MIT Press, 1971. Pp. 569-585.

Ross, R. N. "The coefficient of concordance." *Style*, 1973, 7, 1-20.

Ross, R. N. "Conceptual network analysis." *Semiotica*, 1974, *10*, 1-17.

CHAPTER 5

Poetry Therapy in Private Practice: An Odyssey into the Healing Power of Poetry

Owen E. Heninger

Poetry exposes unconscious forces to consciousness and organizes them into an understandable form. This is a therapeutic process. It makes arrangement out of derangement, harmony out of disharmony, and order out of chaos.

Poetry provides a camouflage that allows the writer (and reader) to ventilate unacceptable, emotionally laden ideas and unconscious conflicts. It allows these ideas and conflicts to circumvent the usual repressive barriers and come to the surface. At the same time, it exposes them to the observing ego so that they can be examined and organized.

There is a clarity that comes from poetry. This clarity is akin to insight. With poetry, one can see more into oneself and become more intimately acquainted with one's own unconscious ideas and feelings. Poetry can provide a more honest way of looking at personal conflicts.

When emotions such as anger and rage cannot be expressed, they lead to symptom formation. When the anger and rage can be expressed in an acceptable manner, the symptoms subside. Venting anger and rage through poetry works to reduce symptoms. It lets off steam, giving an acceptable outlet for explosive forces. Instead of maiming or disfiguring, it releases and soothes. Thus, the process of reading or writing poetry can be seen as a way of coming to terms with one's unconscious, of expressing and venting potentially explosive psychic forces, and of restoring the psychological and physiological balance.

An example of how poetry aids in the healing process is provided by Willa, whom I treated for over five years in private practice. Willa was 46 years old when she came to see me. She had been thoroughly worked up at a large medical clinic for symptoms of recurrent panic, severe headache, crying, nausea, photophobia, dry eyes, and a strong desire for death. No organic basis was found for her symptoms. She sought medical attention and was referred for psychiatric treatment shortly after her 16-year-old daughter Carol was killed in a plane crash.

At the time of her daughter's death, her husband was in a hospital suffering from severe ulcerative colitis and pulmonary embolism and her son was in another hospital with a severely fractured leg. She scarcely cried and barely mourned at the time. She enrolled as a full-time student in a state college, worked toward her teaching credentials and began individual psychotherapy on a weekly basis. After several weeks, she improved slightly and seemed to get some help from her studies. She began putting things together by making up pictures for her class on long rolls of butcher paper. Still she had recurrent, strong suicidal tendencies in addition to her initial symptoms. All symptoms became much worse on the anniversaries of her daughter's death.

I suggested that she read some poems relating to death. As a result, her symptoms were somewhat lessened. Meanwhile, I continued individual psychotherapy and a variety of tranquilizers, sedatives, and analgesics. She was also helped by getting a job as an English teacher and was then able to focus on writing, reading, and reacting to poetry. She wrote a poem about her daughter's death and said it made her feel better. But her symptoms persisted. During this time, her husband had a colectomy for his ulcerative colitis.

She began to express heavily veiled anger toward her husband's brother. He had frequently taken advantage of her husband and often seemed to edge him out of a favored sibling position. Unbeknownst to Willa and her husband, he had enticed their daughter Carol to go flying with him. They had crashed into the sea. He miraculously escaped injury but Carol sank to her death.

Willa frequently alluded to this incident but was not able to verbalize her great anger and hatred. Then she wrote what she could not speak, turning repulsive, odious thoughts into a becoming and presentable poem.

He began in small ways,
He plied the other with mispronunciations
        to confuse him.
He dangled him at the end of hyperbole,
To make his own smallness seem great.

He demanded golden apples while the other
        handled squash.
His wizened brain fevered for Persephone
        while the other chased Athene
He rose like Daedalus on waxen wings,
        and fell.
Then grasped the bark of the other to make
        his way through the deep.

The other planned the sail with a steady
        hand, and made good things grow;
        and honed his tools to make ready
        for life.

While eating crusts, he spread a crystal
table,
And all did think, "What a fine fellow."
The other ate simpler but strong meat,
And did savor the taste as beauty.

He looked upon the other when
both were men.
His emptiness could not be filled
from within,
And he raged with desire,
He reached one day into the vineyard
of the other,
And plucked the choicest fruit,
And soared into the heavens to
satiate his thirst.
He wrung from it all joy and
sweetness, then dropped it,
dead into a well.
The other died while living, and
tried to live while dying.

So he built a plastic dome over
his head
To keep the birds from picking
out his eyes.

She wrote an accompanying letter:

> After putting it on paper, I went through great turmoil over exposing my hatred. I cannot reconcile this with "agape" love which says, "I love you whether you love me or not." Perhaps that is why the names are not there. I hide behind the anonymity and only you and Loren know who "he" is and who "the other is." Sometimes "the other" is Loren, sometimes me, and sometimes both of us. For all the 24 hours of guilt, I feel a sense of satisfaction—a sort of purging since getting this much out—I think there is more—when I can afford the upheaval it causes in me, to write it down.

After a short-lived improvement, Willa developed back pains that led to referral for orthopedic evaluation. The orthopedic workup indicated findings strongly suggestive of a lumbar disc syndrome. She was hospitalized briefly for traction, which gave some relief.

Her husband had started psychotherapy with a psychologist and she then joined him for conjoint therapy. Still her symptoms persisted. Her headaches became so severe that she was referred for a neurosurgical evaluation, which ruled out a brain tumor.

At this point, she and her husband attended a three-day career development planning program. Her symptoms persisted. She saw other doctors, tried many other kinds of medication, wrote more poetry, and started in group therapy. Her symptoms persisted.

She wrote a letter to her mother in which she reviewed some of her own development:

> I did excel in areas of speech and conduct. I became a perfectionist in language and verbal skill . . . when Carol died the whole idea of death became an obsession. It offered a release from the struggle of living without her . . . I guess I vicariously experienced a freedom from my limited "space" for living life—in her. Since she is gone my freedom is gone . . . death seems the only way to a release from the struggle.

Then she and her husband planned a move to another state. Her son, the only remaining child, was helping them move. He was pulling their trailer loaded with household goods when it caught fire and they lost all of their personal possessions. Still, they planned to continue their move and took a scheduled trip to Europe in the interim. On the day they were to return, her minister called me. Willa's son had run over his three-year-old son (her only grandchild, Jerry), killing him. The minister was to meet them at the airport with the sad news. They were to leave immediately for the funeral. I recommended that she write out her feelings.

Two weeks later, I received 11 pages of prose and poetry that led me to weep as I read it. She described her anguish, bewilderment, wild aching, and deep sense of loss. She described feeling an almost inconsolable grief, emptiness, longing, regret and fear. In part she wrote:

> Inside of me a slow release, pent up for eight years, began to gradually break loose—slowly, so slowly—but mixed with the depths of the moment. In those last fifteen hours I had wept an age of dammed up tears. I sobbed heart against heart with my dear Jon, our dear Susan, my beloved Loren and with an ever widening circle of close friends and acquaintances of Jerry, Jon, and Susan. With each embrace, each touch of the hand, the mingling of tears, there flowed together those meant for Carol—so long overdue—and those that came so freely with this poignant hour. As each tide of tears and sorrow enveloped me, it washed out with it some of the anguish— and each time left a greater measure of peace and resolution.

> Like Coventry, the classic yet contemporary beauty and light of Jerry's life and death has been linked/joined with the shattered ruins of that day of devastation (eight years before). Now, at last both mind and heart can comprehend the healing reality of concept of reconciliation, and I am more and more aware of the long awaited sweet peace with God, and a sense of the freedom that comes with forgiveness. I can stand in retrospect and see the rubble created by Carol's accident, but also finally look ahead with my spirit and my senses vibrant with the rich meaning of these hours . . . I have joined the inseparable partnership of sorrow and mingled joy. The struggle is ended. I am bathed in peace.

The crying, so long withheld after Carol's death, was finally loosed and Willa's writing described and facilitated the process.

JERRY HEALER
In these three years you lived
      your destined life.
You made the tarnished sun
      to shine anew;
Shine bright with golden laughter,
      sun-soaked plans
Released long choked springs
      and let them flow
With joy. You salvaged life
      from rushing tangled snare
Of avalanche of fear,
      of fright, of fire.

When flowers bloom again,
      the silenced birds
With you will soar
      and sing your sunshine songs.
The tears will dry.
The sorrow fall away,
      and I will soar and sing
Set free
With you.

The putting together that had been evidenced several years before with pictures on butcher paper for her students had finally been accomplished in a poem. Willa could see into herself. By means of writing poetry, she clarified how Jerry had helped her back from the despair of Carol's death. She could see how his tragic death had somehow opened the floodgates and allowed her to mourn not only his death but the death of her daughter some eight years before. She could examine how her response to Jerry's life and death freed her from the oppression and torture that had so long haunted her after her daughter's death.

Since then Willa has been much relieved and relatively symptom free. She no longer suffers from panic or dry eyes. She no longer takes medication, though she keeps a prescription available, calling it "my security blanket." She has a zest for life and often meets distressing events by writing poetry.

Willa continues psychotherapy with a psychiatrist near her new home and writes of the coming death of her mother-in-law,

> The chain reaction to her death is not happy to contemplate—and the feelings are so strong that I have been experiencing annoying physical symptoms—to say nothing of depression. Dr. A. is really fine and is opening new insights to help me resolve the problems which cause the pain . . . at least to come to terms with them . . . poetry has opened a gift that has made a way for me to live again . . . early on you sent me back to poetry I had read and I came angrily back to you with Tennyson's "In Memorian." After a week of silent anguished sobbing grief (three years after Carol died). Reading this long eulogy opened the flood gates and let me experience in a supportive atmosphere, then—what I was unable to experience at the time. It was the beginning of healing.

In Willa's own words the healing power of poetry,

> . . . reaffirms my faith in my own work to read that others have been sensitive to the same feelings I feel and have used different words and forms to express the same experience.

When her father died, she did not respond with depression. Rather, she was exultant at being able to "sing at his funeral." She talks of both her daughter's death and her father's presence when she writes:

> *The shadow that surrounded all my ways,*
> *Emanating subtle, silent fear,*
> *To censor thoughts and movements, choices, days,*
> *Is gone.*
> *He went away. He left this year.*
>
> *I know the moment he arose*
>   *withdrew*
> *I felt the fettered shackles*
>   *gently move.*
> *I opened windows*

deeply breathed,
and knew
Intoxicating freedom!
Guilt mixed love!

The song welled up,
broke loose my fenced mind.
Release!
for him
for me. Unmeasured joy.
For him from silent darkness—memory;
For me from weighted voice and hand,
his ploy
That silenced lovely songs,
and created dreams.

Today my eyes sow sky,
white clouds, the shore,
Felt cooling zephyrs gently
touch my cheek.
Elysian fields now mine to roam,
explore,
While he, new worlds
on Mt. Olympus seeks.

Thus, Willa came to acceptable terms with living by facing her deeper problems and conflicts. She ventilated her insufferable anger and resolved her psychic dilemmas by organizing and arranging them in a poetic form. Willa's experience is a good example of an odyssey into the healing power of poetry.

CHAPTER 6

Poetry Therapy in the Psychiatric Hospital

Allan S. Abrams

Introduction

In the following discussion I shall present what I have learned from my personal, relatively recent experiences with poetry and poetry therapy in relation to the psychiatric hospital.

My first encounter with poetry therapy occurred several years ago, shortly after I became clinical program director in Woodview-Calabasas Psychiatric Hospital. Participating and observing poetry therapy sessions directed by Dr. Arthur Lerner soon resolved my initial skepticism and led me to consider with great interest many questions regarding the therapeutic effects of poetry. My dual role of psychiatric administrator and, subsequently, poetry therapy advisor gave me an opportunity to evaluate the relationship between poetry therapy and the psychiatric hospital. I discovered that this relationship includes the often cool pragmatism of the hospital's administrative and political machinery, the hospital's role as a place of healing, and the almost transcendental spirit of the art of poetry.

Historical and Philosophical Antecedents

During the past century, a growing recognition of the benefits of good literature as an aid to patient recovery spread to hospitals. The formalization of concepts and techniques for using books increased as therapy grew into bibliotherapy, which was the foundation of poetry therapy.

The historic origins of poetry therapy reach back to about 330 B.C. when Aristotle authored the first analysis of the art of poetry (Butcher, 1907). He believed that literature and other arts aroused emotions within a person in such a

63

way as to have beneficial effects. For example, he wrote of the *katharsis* or purgation of the feelings of pity and fear latent in the spectator of a tragic drama. He pointed out that it is release of these emotions which brings pleasure to the spectators. In his time, meaningful views of the human condition were presented in the form of poetic dramas which creatively imitated the universal elements of human life. He viewed the concept of the ideal as the real freed from alien influence and chance, thus able to follow a natural development from beginning to end. It is interesting that this view parallels today's thought of how psychotherapy frees up natural psychological development from the stifling and self-defeating influences of internal conflicts.

The first known use of poetry with mental hospital patients was recorded in the late 18th century at the Pennsylvania Hospital in Philadelphia (Jones, 1969). This institution was the first hospital in the American colonies to care for the mentally ill. Here, Benjamin Rush, the father of American psychiatry, introduced the adjunctive therapies of music and literature to psychiatric patients. In the mid-19th century, John M. Galt, a psychiatrist at the mental hospital in Williamsburg, Virginia, was the first American to publish a book on the therapeutic nature of library services for the mentally ill. As a result, there was a great expansion of libraries in mental hospitals throughout the United States.

Changes occurred in the early mental hospitals where beating, straight-jackets, ostracism, dispossession, and many other forms of abuse and neglect were common. There arose an experimental attitude seeking to find methods which undermined regressive impulses and promoted new ways of eliciting human energy and potential toward improved adjustment and healing (Green-blatt, York, & Brown, 1955).

Thus, as man's thinking on the nature of man began to include the psyche's inner dimensions, the mentally ill came to be seen in a more humane light. The understanding of literature and its impact upon men evolved to new clarity. It was the growing awareness of this inner dimension, and literature's ability to shed light on it, that led to new methods for psychological healing, such as bibliotherapy. Bibliotherapy, as most succinctly defined by psychiatrist Julius Griffin (1972), "is the scientific application of literature toward therapeutic goals."

In 1904 McLean Hospital near Boston opened the first hospital library for the mentally ill where it was recognized that there was an affinity between psychiatry and what was to be labeled "bibliotherapy" by Rev. Samuel Crothers in 1919. The professional literature on bibliotherapy reveals a chronological sequence of deepening understanding, which clearly applies to poetry therapy and in fact became its foundation. It is easily documented that during the previous decades, the therapeutic technique of using literature had slowly grown in definition and description. Psychologist Gerald Lawlor sketched a general rationale for the use of literary works in bibliotherapy. He stated that reading keeps alive the urge to change. Reading stimulates the patient with a continuing flow of ideas regarding new ways of looking at oneself. The patient is encouraged to break through the outer-inner dichotomy and express himself in universal themes as part of this world with its fluidity and change (Leuschner, 1966).

There was resistance to bibliotherapy by the psychiatric establishment. Some professionals believed that only a dyadic psychotherapeutic relationship had any value. Psychiatric advocates of bibliotherapy may have enhanced resistance by erroneous application. For example, one writer recommended the prescription of technical psychiatric literature with the aim of teaching the patient psychological terminology to enable him to communicate better with the therapist (Gottschalk, 1948). As methods of bibliotherapy were explored, it became clear that solitary readings on psychology contributed almost nothing toward the improvement of the mentally ill.

Another therapeutic foundation for poetry therapy was group therapy. In 1919 L. Cody Marsh was the first psychiatrist to apply group therapy to hospitalized psychiatric patients (Alexander & Selesnick, 1966, pp. 334-335). At New York's Cumberland Hospital in 1959, Eli Greifer started the first psychiatric hospital poetry therapy group, assisted by Dr. Samuel Spector and Dr. Jack Leedy (Leedy, 1969).

Current Concepts

Poetry therapy in a psychiatric hospital is concerned with helping people who have severe problems with living. It is good to keep in mind that abnormality is, in essence, a destructively exaggerated state of normality and normal psychological processes. Nearly everyone experiences depressive feelings, paranoid thoughts, and regressive impulses at times. While the use of poetry for therapeutic ends grew out of its popular use, knowledge of the therapeutic techniques of poetry therapy came from the study of abnormality. It has been the study of the severely disturbed that has brought us knowledge and understanding of normality. The effectiveness of poetry with the severely disturbed led us to know how powerful it can be with the average person.

Recent literature has clarified the relationship between poetry and psychotherapy. Lawler (1972) succinctly described how poetry provides insights into the human condition and, by proper application, insights by the patient into his own condition. The patient responds to poetry dealing with a lesser level of development or adjustment in himself. The anxiety thereby produced tends to motivate him toward functioning at a higher level. In a seminal article on the poetic process and psychotherapy, psychoanalyst Albert Rothenberg (1972) discussed the role of psychological freedom. In the poet's struggle with his psyche he unearths deeper and hidden aspects of himself. The process of successfully creating the poem dealing with these issues leads to relief and resolution. The involved reader also experiences wonder and anxiety about the actual unconscious process revealed. On the one hand, he is relieved and reassured to see that the processes of the poet are similar to his. On the other hand, the reader is both threatened and stimulated to think about the conflicts in himself and perhaps to work on them. This work leads not only to greater self-definition but also to a clearer view of the world: "All great art is anxiety provoking" (Rothenberg, 1972, p. 253).

A Particular Poetry Therapy Program

In this section I shall give a description of the particular poetry therapy program I have been involved with in its relationship to Woodview-Calabasas Psychiatric Hospital, a private 80-bed hospital in Calabasas, California. It sits on a bluff amidst rolling hills at the west end of the San Fernando Valley near Los Angeles. From the time the hospital first opened in 1971, clinical psychologist and poet Dr. Arthur Lerner has directed a program for poetry therapy. His program got off to an exuberant start. It included regular meetings with patients as well as readings and sessions involving the participation of people from outside the institution. However, in 1972 and 1973 there were several dramatic and significant changes in the administrative structure of the hospital.

Because of these changes, the poetry therapy program continued in an atmosphere of great uncertainty. This period of change saw an entire medical staff organization of over 100 psychiatrists and new administrative and treatment personnel transfer from another hospital. The proprietary nature of the hospital's existence and new administrative control changed the financial footing of the poetry therapy program. Instead of being a part of the milieu, available to all patients who could use it or were interested, poetry therapy became a specialized adjunctive program for which a separate fee was charged (not usually covered by the patient's insurance). Moreover, the poetry therapy had to be specifically prescribed by the patient's doctors in a hospital with a psychiatric attending staff and administration unaware of the healing potential of poetry therapy. There was uncertainty about the value of Dr. Lerner's group. As a new program director, I was drawn by curiosity and skepticism to observe his meetings. My appreciation and understanding grew as I attended more meetings. Since then, I have met regularly with Dr. Lerner and his staff to exchange and evaluate ideas.

As the program presently exists, two one-hour group meetings are held one evening each week in coordination with other treatment program activities. Patient attendance in each group averages about eight to ten. Attending each meeting are the poetry therapy director, three poetry therapy facilitators (from the Poetry Therapy Institute, in nearby Encino, California), and at least one member of the hospital milieu therapy staff. The role of the director is to guide the group toward open discussion of various psychological issues (such as frustration, loss, self-respect, and dependency) raised by patients.

The poetry therapy director reads, or prescribes for reading to the group, specific poems which he judges relevant to the patients' area of conflict and which may be supportive or insight promoting. The facilitators echo this role with poem suggestions and discussion in support of themes raised by the poetry therapy director or themes they themselves perceive as relevant. The milieu staff person, usually a psychiatric aide, is free to work as a facilitator along with his primary role of providing any needed structure and supervision of patients. The aide (with other nursing personnel) is also responsible for coordinating the attendance of patients in this activity at the scheduled time and for maintaining communication between the patient, hospital staff, and poetry therapist. For example, a particular patient may have had a strong reaction to a certain idea in psychodrama earlier in the day. This information will be communicated to the poetry therapy director prior to his session. My role is to observe group meetings and group process so as to be of help in the post-group discussion.

Usually, referral to the poetry therapy program is made on the basis of such factors as the patient's emotional and mental organization, which will insure his ability to participate in the session. Attendance at the sessions is prescribed or denied for each patient at the time of hospital admission or at one of the twice-weekly staff conferences held to maintain clear communication between the attending psychiatrist and the hospital treatment staff. The analysis and formulation of each patient's psychodynamics is the basis of specific treatment plans. Awareness of these dynamic factors (the external and intrapsychic forces acting on the patient's situation) permits flexibility and current awareness of progress or lack of progress.

Philosophical and Practical Variations in Psychiatric Hospitals

A relatively recent innovation, which is transforming psychiatric hospitals into truly growth-stimulating institutions, is the concept of the therapeutic community or reactive environment. Here there is much greater responsibility for treatment placed on the treatment staff and patients. In the past quarter century, because of the pioneering influence of Maxwell Jones (1953), Stanton and Schwartz (1954), and others, it has been increasingly recognized that all staff members play a significant role in making therapy effective in the psychiatric hospital. The traditional medical autocracy persists in the more subtle form of such attitudes as seeing the doctor-patient relationship as the only vital one in the patient's treatment. The doctor's legal responsibility for the patient's treatment is often used to rationalize a depreciation of the therapeutic involvement of others (Maxmen, Tucker, & LeBow, 1974). My own experience has dealt with the difficulty encountered by office-based private psychiatrists in opening to the team approach so necessary to hospital psychiatric treatment. All treatment staff who interact with the patient during the day play an important role in planning and implementing a treatment program. With the increasing recognition of the importance of the overall hospital environment, the role of the adjunctive therapies, such as poetry therapy, has become more accepted and potentially more effective.

The concept of the therapeutic community embraces a subtle balance of structured authority and creative openness. The milieu must be so structured that people with emotional and mental troubles feel that it is safe to openly express their feelings. The milieu staff must have enough teamwork, competence, and human awareness to be able to respond in a helpful way to the behavioral and verbal expressions of these feelings. In part, the success of a poetry therapy program depends on how well the milieu staff is educated in the philosophy of poetry therapy. Certainly, there must be some degree of understanding to prevent rivalry among the various therapies practiced in a psychiatric hospital.

In the context of the therapeutic community/reactive environment, the specialized technique of poetry therapy offers the patient an additional perspective or approach from which needed insight or emotional release may result. However, this technique is clearly an adjunctive therapy. It is an integral part of the therapeutic program system rather than the system itself: "A tool rather than a school" (Lerner, 1973, p. 1337). Adjunctive therapies, such as poetry, art, dance, and recreation therapies, offer mutually reinforcing methods for eliciting a patient's individuality.

There are some difficulties inherent in the introduction of a new poetry therapy program. Initiating a new program, as with any change in a social pattern, means encountering temporary resistance. This must be dealt with effectively lest it become chronic. The poetry therapist must be open to administrative political realities. He must attempt to be aware of and understand the feelings of administrators, psychiatrists, and hospital treatment personnel. There are often doubts, fears, and hostility about the new program. For example, there might be concern that the poetry therapy program will conflict with the overall treatment program or that the poetry therapist lacks therapeutic discipline and technique. Most commonly, and sadly, there may be no feeling about the efficacy of poetry therapy. Resistance, as in therapy itself, must be understood as fear and dealt with in a positive manner.

Some Comments on Poetry Versus Therapy

It must be remembered that a poet, by the nature of his creative skill, is a natural opponent to the "system." The iconoclastic free spirit must be disciplined or workably contained in order to apply the tool of poetry therapy. Those who use this tool must be open, both in terms of the milieu in which they work and the framework of therapeutic technique. Diplomatic skills are indispensable.

Poetry therapy, which is a whole dimension beyond writing or reading poetry, takes the rational effort of the psychotherapist to understand what is going on. This understanding is what determines technique in the group sessions. An adequate degree of training in psychotherapeutic and group process is essential for the poetry therapist. The psychodynamic model of these processes offers a method of thinking about and communicating what is occurring in people's interactions. The technique of psychotherapy involves the synthesis of an intervention based on the perceptions and inner responses of the therapist to verbal and nonverbal behavior of the patient. Intervention refers to an interpretation, suggestion, confrontation, or other response of the therapist with a specific therapeutic goal.

There are two types of attitudes for the therapist to cultivate and maintain. First, an inner-directed self-awareness and openness is necessary in order to monitor internal reactions to the patient. The therapist's reactions to the patient are often the most meaningful clues to the patient's emotional state. For example, one young woman seduced the entire group into listening to her dramatic descriptions of an exciting life. It was when she deftly avoided reading deep, sad poems and revealed, cheerfully and in passing, that she was in the hospital for a suicide attempt following abandonment by her lover, that her seductive defenses against resolving her grief became apparent. The goal is to clarify for the patient what exists in his feelings, attitudes, and blind spots so he gains freedom of choice in his life. In the above example, the patient needed relief from her need to seduce—that is, relief of her fear and flight from sadness—before she could resolve her problems further.

The second attitude of concern for the therapist is that of emotional separateness. The more open the therapist is to himself, the more clearly he can differentiate between his own and the patient's feelings, and the more therapeutic he can be. He is then more able to see himself as a separate person while maintaining empathy for the patient's experience. This *empathic separateness* is a quality to be cultivated. Thus, the poetry therapist must not only trigger insights with poems about the patient's internal conflict but must also be able to maintain a positive, active relationship without being manipulated or overwhelmed by the patient's disturbed feelings. Another way of putting it is that training in self-awareness helps the therapist avoid expressing natural impulses and reactions which might counteract the patient's gaining and using insight. Empathic separateness permits and facilitates the nonjudgmental neutrality necessary for effective therapeutic interventions.

Educational and Training Potential for Poetry Therapy in the Psychiatric Hospital

Edgar and Hazley (1969) have proposed a poetry therapy curriculum for which the hospital setting offers potential fulfillment. After didactic preparation, they recommend an internship in which the therapy student observes and performs poetry therapy under supervision.

The psychiatric hospital has been a primary site for training in psycho-pathology and psychotherapy for a long time. As a training ground, it offers some distinct advantages for poetry therapy. First, there is the availability of an abundant amount of clinical material. Direct exposure to patients with a wide variety of emotional and mental disorders (in living, breathing, and painful reality) is an experience infinitely superior to reading descriptions of diagnostic labels in a textbook of abnormal psychology. Secondly, the hospital offers a protected environment with readily available supportive personnel. The student therapist is free to work on understanding and learning in an already structured and scheduled program rather than facing alone what is invariably an anxiety-provoking situation. Exposure to people whose defenses have failed and whose primitive feelings and impulses are less controlled and more openly expressed can arouse a deep fear of the same thing happening in an untrained observer. I believe it is this deep fear of losing one's control (losing one's integrated self) that is most threatening to those not used to dealing with people who have severe emotional and mental disorders. Active supervision and support within the hospital milieu thus assists the control of anxiety that makes learning possible. Another advantage common to the hospital setting is exposure to different therapeutic disciplines. Ultimately, every therapist must synthesize a basically consistent style of technique which best utilizes his unique personal strengths. The experience of several forms of therapy in the hospital offers choices and flexibility which help prevent dogmatism and stagnation. The hospital setting also facilitates the poetry therapist's understanding that his role is one among many important roles in the patient's hospital care. This helps lessen the tendency, found in therapists of every discipline, to adopt a self-aggrandizing attitude which, in the short term, may be personally gratifying to the therapist but is often therapeutically harmful to the patient.

Conclusion

Briefly, the place of poetry therapy in a psychiatric hospital seems to be that of a highly compatible member of the hospital's treatment team. However, the prospective poetry therapist should be aware of some of the problems experienced in psychiatric institutions. As the situation presently stands, the existence of well-organized programs of poetry therapy remains relatively infrequent in psychiatric hospitals. Nonetheless, the validity of poetry therapy, its usefulness, and the unique nature of its approach have become increasingly clear. Thus, the present process of change toward more therapeutically active hospital treatment programs represents a fertile ground for future growth.

References

Alexander, Franz G., & Selesnick, Sheldon T. *The history of psychiatry: An evaluation of psychiatric thought and practice from prehistoric times to the present*. New York: Harper, 1966.

Aristotle's theory of poetry and fine art. Translated by S. H. Butcher. New York: Dover, 1907.

Edgar, K. P., & Hazley, R. "A curriculum proposal for training poetry therapists." In *Poetry therapy*. Jack J. Leedy (Ed.), Philadelphia: Lippincott, 1969. Pp. 260-268.

Gottschalk, Louis A. "Bibliotherapy as an adjunct to psychotherapy." *American Journal of Psychiatry*, 1948, *104*, 632-637.

Greenblatt, Milton, York, Richard H., & Brown, Esther Lucile, in collaboration with Robert W. Hyde. *From custodial care to therapeutic patient care in mental hospitals*. New York: Russell Sage Foundation, 1955.

Griffin, Julius. From a paper presented to a class in "Poetry and the Therapeutic Experience" at University of California Extension, Los Angeles, May 9, 1972.

Jones, Maxwell. *The therapeutic community: A new treatment method in psychiatry*. New York: Basic Books, 1953.

Jones, Robert E. "Treatment of a psychotic patient by poetry therapy." In Jack J. Leedy (Ed.), *Poetry therapy*. Philadelphia: Lippincott, 1969.

Lawler, Justus G. "Poetic therapy?" *Psychiatry*, 1972, *35*, 227-237.

Leedy, Jack J. "Introduction." In Jack J. Leedy (Ed.), *Poetry therapy*. Philadelphia: Lippincott, 1969. Pp. 11-13.

Lerner, Arthur. "Poetry therapy." *American Journal of Nursing*, 1973, *73*, 1336-1338.

Leuschner, Lucille K. "Bibliotherapy and patient libraries: The growth of hospital library services." In Gerald O'Morrow (Ed.), *Administration of activity therapy service*. Springfield, Ill.: Thomas, 1966. Pp. 137-172.

Maxmen, Jerrold S., Tucker, Gary J., & LeBow, Michael D. *Rational hospital psychiatry: The reactive environment*. New York: Brunner/Mazel, 1974.

Rothenberg, Albert. "Poetic process and psychotherapy." *Psychiatry*, 1972, *35*, 228-254.

Stanton, A. H., & Schwartz, M. S. *The mental hospital: A study of institutional participation in psychiatric illness and treatment*. New York: Basic Books, 1954.

CHAPTER 7

Abuses of Poetry Therapy

Roger Lauer

There is nothing so true that the damps of error have not warped it.
Martin Tupper

Half the truth will very often amount to absolute falsehood.
Richard Whately

Therapy denotes a procedure to prevent or alter an ailment (see Feinstein, 1967, pp. 231-246), and poetry, taken broadly, refers to writing that appears as spontaneous, graceful, expressive and beautiful. Poetry therapy can then be defined as a method of treating emotional disturbances in which beautiful writing is listened to and/or created. When poetry is used for purposes other than for treating ailments (as in recreation, teaching, or religious worship), the term "poetry therapy" would not apply.

Poetry therapy, like any other treatment method, can be used poorly and improperly. Such abuse is not merely hypothetical, since misapplications and corruptions of poetry therapy have already occurred. This chapter will delineate three interrelated types of abuse and suggest some safeguards.

The abuses to be delineated are that poetry therapy has been used primarily to express practitioner zeal, has been applied indiscriminately, and has been proferred by incompetents. My opinions result from interactions with poetry therapists across the United States, from personal experiences as a poetry therapist, and from my past research into the merits of various folk methods of treatment (Ilfeld & Lauer, 1964; Lauer, 1973a, 1973b, 1974).

72

Fanaticism

Some people can't practice poetry therapy rationally because of extreme fervor. They seek attention and converts with fixed, unproven ideas, with unrestrained, unrealistic claims, and with ballyhoo, particularly sensational publicity in the general media. They forsake other kinds of personal and professional activities. They abuse poetry therapy by making it a consuming passion, a faith, an ideology, a dogma, and a crusade rather than just a treatment method.

Case Example: Edwin Malley

(In this and subsequent cases, changes have been made to disguise identities.)

Edwin Malley, 45 years old, originally had studied for the priesthood but then became skeptical about doctrine and left the church to work as a social worker in a Boston drug abuse clinic. He was bored and frustrated with his job until a newspaper article about poetry therapy stimulated him to experiment by reading poems to a group of his clients. The group members seemed pleased, excited, and "turned on" by the activity. Mr. Malley also enjoyed it, feeling that poetry therapy enabled him to make "real" contact with his clients.

Mr. Malley's enthusiasm grew. He believed that poetry therapy could not only alleviate psychological distress but also could cure such physical problems as ulcers, asthma, and hypertension. Furthermore, it could lead generally to peace, contentment, and happiness. To him, poetry therapy was a "boon to mankind." He talked about such matters with single-minded intensity and discussed little else. Friends and colleagues were surprised at his preoccupation but tolerated it as a harmless eccentricity.

Mr. Malley went beyond his own social circle to spread the word and encouraged strangers to experience poetry therapy both as patients and therapists. He organized public demonstrations of the method, wrote and distributed press releases, arranged interviews, cultivated contacts with media people, and relentlessly tried to secure publicity on radio, TV, newspapers, and national magazines. Such proselytizing came easy to Mr. Malley, as he was a persuasive speaker and a good salesman. It also was gratifying for he felt that his cause was noble and righteous, and he enjoyed generating stories and receiving attention.

Discussion

Mental health practitioners have often responded with initial bursts of enthusiasm to treatment innovations and only later formed more measured views. Examples of innovations that have prompted such changes in attitudes include cocaine, electroshock, psychosurgery, and psychoanalysis. Many practitioners, including myself, have followed this same pattern in regard to poetry therapy: early excitement gave way to calm, objective appraisal. Others, however, have followed a different course, going from enthusiasm to passionate avowal. They became fanatics; as with other "true believers" (Hoffer, 1951), the focus of their fervor was often less important than their having a grand passion.

Many of these poetry therapy fanatics saw themselves not as isolated workers but as members of on ongoing school of poetry therapy which was destined to receive widespread acclaim. They derived encouragement and support from unity with this community of believers. Securing new adherents helped bolster unrealistic, unproved beliefs. By convincing outsiders of the wonders of their faith, they convinced themselves. Group support and proselytizing served a psychologically defensive function or, to use Festinger's (1957) term, reduced "cognitive dissonance."

In my opinion, poetry therapists should cultivate a sober, rational attitude, delineate explicitly and carefully the nature of their work, insist on being grounded in facts and scientific data, maintain professional standards, and discourage impassioned rhetoric, dogma, and cultism. They should be humble about their powers, have sensible, modest expectations about the results of their efforts, and view poetry therapy more as a form of psychotherapy than as a mystical experience or a healing-religious ritual. Dr. Arthur Lerner encapsulated this viewpoint when he called poetry therapy "a tool, not a school."

The Panacea

Certain practitioners hold that poetry therapy is good for whatever ails you. Regardless of the presenting problem, it helps everyone quickly, easily, and painlessly (for discussion of psychological factors involved in this viewpoint see Vanderpool, 1973). In addition, enthusiasts may view other treatment methods as less potent or even valueless, and therefore neither worthy alternatives nor supplements to poetry therapy. Drugs, electroshock, and other somatic treatment methods have been particularly scorned by these enthusiasts and have been labeled quackery, oppression, or torture. In short, some practitioners feel that poetry therapy has broad spectrum benefits, no dangers, and clear superiority over other methods.

From this it follows that screening of clients is unnecessary. A "come one, come all" approach can be taken and customers recruited indiscriminately. Another argument is sometimes raised: since clients ultimately choose whether or not to participate in poetry therapy, they consequently must take personal responsibility for their decision. In other words, blanket recruitment is justified by the doctrine of *caveat emptor*.

Case Example: Russell Howard

Russell Howard, a 30-year-old married biology instructor with a 3-year-old son moved to the suburbs of Washington, D.C., for a new job in a junior college. With his intelligence, ambition, and ability he seemed to have a promising career ahead of him, but was troubled regarding his identity. Occasionally, he would show bizarre behavior for a few days, especially when under stress. He might be unrealistically suspicious of his wife's fidelity, or preoccupied with theology and metaphysics, but then would quickly snap back to his usual self.

The chairman of the biology department, an unpublished poet, was enthralled with poetry therapy, although possessing only a nebulous conception of what it involved. He pushed Mr. Howard to enter a poetry therapy group so as to unleash his creativity, but he neglected to assess Mr. Howard's personal needs and his likely response to such a therapy group. The clinical psychologist leading the group likewise did little to evaluate Mr. Howard's suitability for poetry therapy.

Mr. Howard entered the group hoping to decrease his inner turmoil, but the group experience made him even more upset. As he was pressed to examine himself, important psychological defenses were breached. He dredged up strange, threatening ideas which were frightening and overwhelming, yet hypnotically fascinating. Both his department chairman and his therapist were pleased by his emotional arousal, thinking it confirmed the value of his treatment. They encouraged him to participate in more sessions so as to make "further progress."

Mr. Howard subsequently became grossly disturbed, grandiose, paranoid, and disorganized. He lost his job, left his wife, shaved off the hair on his head and body, symbolically tried to change himself by changing his name, claimed he was God and could read minds, and eventually wandered the streets babbling incoherently. He had a florid psychotic break, which in retrospect seemed to have been triggered in part by his poetry therapy. Mr. Howard was later hospitalized in several mental institutions and treated with antipsychotic medication but he did not regain his previous level of functioning. One year after the onset of his illness he solved his difficulties once and for all by killing himself.

Discussion

It is difficult to predict whether a given patient will benefit from poetry therapy or, for that matter, from any form of psychotherapy. Many commentators have noted that psychotherapy effectiveness rests upon the client's having an underlying sympathy toward the method. Torrey (1972, p. 172) stated that client and therapist must share a world view. To Frank (1973, p. 325), a client must be able to make sense of the treatment and believe in it. Yalom (1975) said that a client must see relevant satisfactions in treatment. By this line of reasoning, clients for poetry therapy should be selected on the basis of leaning toward the method. Granted that they initially may well be hesitant or resistant, they should show promise of being comfortable eventually in the treatment activity. On the other hand, a person with an unyielding negative attitude, such as the unshakable conviction that poetry is effeminate, would not be a good candidate for poetry therapy.

The overall treatment context can influence whether a person benefits from poetry therapy. Patients receiving poetry therapy alone seem to do less well than those who simultaneously receive additional treatment, such as traditional psychotherapy, medication, vocational counseling, or hospitalization (Lauer & Goldfield, 1970). In my opinion, poetry therapy is best used as an ancillary technique to other approaches and as part of a comprehensive treatment program, not as an isolated effort that is expected to provide complete aid. A similar opinion has been expressed by Berger (in Leedy, 1969, p. 75).

Particularly likely candidates for poetry therapy would include the following who are faced with certain kinds of presenting problems: (1) persons who feel inhibited or frustrated about self-expression, who may even have artistic abilities and goals, and who need encouragement, stimulation, and nurturance; (2) persons who are lonely, withdrawn, and alienated and who misunderstand the conventions of American society and find social interaction difficult—some young adult drug abusers fit into this category (Goldfield & Lauer, 1971); (3) persons who seem stiff, rigid, and inflexible because of stereotyped, maladaptive behavior but who can tolerate exploring alternative paths of action (Lauer, 1972); (4) persons at an impasse in psychotherapy but who may be able to move forward if stimulated by a new treatment activity.

Determining who will benefit from poetry therapy is difficult; so is determining who will be harmed by it. Bergin (Bergin & Garfield, 1971, p. 250), in reviewing the scant literature on deterioration during psychotherapy, forlornly concluded that additional research is urgently needed. Hadley and Strupp (1976) surveyed practitioners for their views regarding negative effects of psychotherapy. Yalom (1975, p. 221) suggested that patients who are brain damaged, paranoid, extremely narcissistic, hypochondriacal, suicidal, addicted to drugs or alcohol, acutely psychotic, or sociopathic are poor candidates for intensive outpatient group therapy, although some such patients might respond to specialized forms of group therapy. With respect to poetry therapy specifically, more attention has been paid to how harm might be caused than to who might be a greatest risk. Rothenberg (1972, p. 31) has written that poetry can divert problems, produce severe conflicts, and support maladaptive behavior. Pattison (in Leedy, 1973) has pointed out that either patient or therapist can use poetry defensively.

There is reason to believe that poetry therapy presents special risks to schizophrenics and therefore should be used cautiously. People with acute schizophrenia cannot process and integrate stimuli normally and may be very sensitive to environmental events (Van Putten, 1973). Ideally, they should reside in a quiet, peaceful, nonthreatening setting where the reduced stimulus input helps them to strengthen psychological defenses, reduce mental imagery, and control expressive behavior. Poetry therapy may aggravate their mental disorder by serving to confuse, disturb, and overwhelm. For persons with chronic or borderline schizophrenia, the issue is similar. These people tend to have brittle psychological defenses, little ability to tolerate stress, and a vulnerability to acute breakdown. Their mental condition could be worsened by any psychotherapeutic technique, including poetry therapy, that was used in an aggressive, intrusive fashion (see Yalom & Lieberman, 1971).

Since poetry therapy is not altogether harmless, clients should weigh the dangers and make rational, informed choices about undertaking it. However, because of naivete or impaired judgment, they may be unable to do so and may need aid and protection. It is the therapist's responsibility to provide this. He should judge whether the case fits his competence and whether poetry therapy is the best possible procedure. He should work toward the client's best interests, encouraging whatever treatment is appropriate and not blindly urging poetry therapy. In short, a poetry therapist should act as a professional therapist and not as a salesman.

The Anyone-Can-Do-It Approach

Some poetry therapists claim their work to be so easy that qualifications are unnecessary. They view all members of the general public as capable of doing it and issue blanket appeals for recruits. They believe that formal training, therapeutic skill, and psychological knowledge are not required and may even be liabilities by inhibiting honesty, candor, and spontaneity. They may consider advantageous a desire or calling for the work and a literary background or "love of poetry," but these are not essentials.

Case Example: Rhonda Mullins

In college, Rhonda Mullins had received attention for her good looks and brains. She was popular with both boys and girls, was on the dean's list, and was the editor of the school literary magazine. Years later, at age 44, her earlier bloom had faded. She was a divorced real estate saleswoman who wore bright, short skirts in a desperate attempt to recapture her co-ed career. She found it difficult to fill her free time, rarely received praise or recognition, and felt tired, lonely, depressed, and unfulfilled. Life seemed empty.

A friend who was an avid poetry therapist described the pleasures of her work. She suggested that Mrs. Mullins take it up, claiming her literary experience would be an asset and her lack of background in psychology or psychotherapy would not be a drawback. Stimulated by this suggestion, Mrs. Mullins found a job as a volunteer (nonsalaried) poetry therapist at a suburban mental health center. The center accepted her because it was underfinanced, understaffed, and eager for help of almost any sort.

Mrs. Mullins enjoyed her work, being particularly pleased by the opportunity to read dramatically before groups and to be in the limelight. Her therapeutic goal with patients was "to make them feel." Because she herself delighted in being emotionally stimulated, she thought that others would, too. She drew patients out on matters of personal concern and was pleased when they seemed sad, angry, guilty, envious, or moved in other ways. Afterward, she disengaged since she believed eliciting feelings was a therapeutic end in itself and had no concept of a next step.

However, her patients, most of them with chronic schizophrenia, found it difficult to disengage. They wanted and needed resolution of their emotional arousal. It took many months for Mrs. Mullins to sense this need. Eventually, she tried to meet it by dogmatically giving advice, often couched in platitudes. Doing this was comfortable for her. She liked presenting herself as a sage and telling patients in an authoritarian, domineering way how to solve their problems and how to lead their lives. Some patients appreciated her advice, but others protested the heavy-handed imposition of unacceptable values and ideas.

Emboldened by her seeming success at the mental health center, Mrs. Mullins began making speeches to the general public about her work. On a few occasions, she read her patients' writing, identified them by their correct names, and discussed their personal problems. The patients were unaware of this and had not given permission for it. When questioned, Mrs. Mullins seemed oblivious to the ethical issues involved and to commonly accepted psychotherapeutic principles of confidentiality and informed consent (this issue is discussed in Pearson, 1965, p. 44). In her public presentations, Mrs. Mullins claimed that providing poetry therapy was easy and encouraged people to become poetry therapists. She had done it, so could they.

Discussion

In a sense, it is true that anyone can provide poetry therapy. Since no special permission or authorization is required, anyone is free to call himself a poetry therapist and engage in practice, regardless of competence or qualifications. This lack of regulation has permitted the emergence of poetry therapists who have not understood emotional problems, lacked the skills required to conduct psychotherapy, and had quirks or personal qualities interfering with effective treatments. Some have been frustrated poets and performers searching for audiences or mental patients searching for personal cures. Some have been unethical, irresponsible, exploitative, seductive, histrionic, controlling, or self-aggrandizing.

It seems obvious that not everyone has the skills and personal qualities required to do effective poetry therapy. There may be difficulty in pinpointing the precise requirements, but guidelines are available from the literature on psychotherapy. For example, Truax (in Bergin & Garfield, 1971, p. 310) argued that psychotherapists should possess knowledge concerning normal and pathological behavior, a logically cohesive group of theoretical concepts, experience in therapeutically integrating observations with concepts through clinical work, the ability to grasp empathically what the patient means beyond the face value of his statements, and awareness of their own inner mental processes and their influence on therapeutic techniques.

Poetry therapists, like other psychotherapists, should be carefully screened, trained, and accredited. They should be selected for talent and personal qualities, then taught basic skills and techniques by experienced practitioners. They must learn how to think and work as professionals (Ruesch, 1976, p. 321). Initially, they should be closely supervised. After completing training, they should pass a final evaluation of their competence to practice.

Conclusion

Although poetry therapy can be enjoyable and can prompt psychological change, it is no cure-all. Like virtually all other forms of psychotherapy, it may be useful, irrelevant, or harmful, depending upon the client, his particular difficulty, and the treatment context. Harm is most likely to result when the poetry therapist is incompetent, irresponsible, or poorly trained. The harm can spring from the poetry therapy process itself (such as breaking down needed psychological defenses) or it can come indirectly by sidetracking people from more appropriate treatment. In assessing the suitability of poetry therapy for a given patient, one should realistically decide whether the potential benefits outweigh the hazards.

References

Berger, Irving, L. "Poetry as therapy—therapy as poetry." In Jack Leedy (Ed.), *Poetry therapy*. Philadelphia: Lippincott, 1969. Pp. 75-87.

Bergin, Allen, & Garfield, Sol. *Handbook of psychotherapy and behavior change*. New York: Wiley, 1971.

Colby, Kenneth. *A primer for psychotherapists*. New York: Ronald Press, 1951.

Feinstein, Alan R. *Clinical judgment*. Baltimore: Williams & Wilkins, 1967.

Festinger, Leon. *A theory of cognitive dissonance*. Stanford, Calif.: Stanford University Press, 1957.

Frank, Jerome. *Persuasion and healing*. Rev. Ed. Baltimore: Johns Hopkins University Press, 1973.

Goldfield, Michael, & Lauer, Roger. "The use of creative writing in young adult drug abusers." *The New Physician*, 1971, *20*, 449-457.

Hadley, S., & Strupp, H. "Contemporary views of negative effect in psychotherapy." *Archives of General Psychiatry*, 1976, *33*, 1291-1302.

Hoffer, Eric. *The true believer*. New York: Harper & Row, 1951.

Ilfeld, Fred, & Lauer, Roger. *Social nudism in America*. New Haven, Conn.: College and University Press, 1964.

Lauer, Roger. "Creative writing as a therapeutic tool." *Hospital and Community Psychiatry*, 1972, *23*, 55-56.

Lauer, Roger. "Masters of metaphysics." In Richard Cox (Ed.), *Religious systems and psychotherapy*. Springfield, Ill.: Thomas, 1973a. Pp. 254-267.

Lauer, Roger. "Urban shamans." *The New Physician*, 1973b, *22*, 486-489.

Lauer, Roger. "A medium for mental health." In Irving Zaretsky & Mark Leone (Eds.), *Religious movements in contemporary America*. Princeton: Princeton University Press, 1974. Pp. 338-354.

Lauer, Roger, & Goldfield, Michael. "Creative writing in group therapy." *Psychotherapy: Theory, Research, and Practice*, 1970, *7*, 248-252.

Leedy, Jack (Ed.) *Poetry therapy*. Philadelphia: Lippincott, 1969.

Leedy, Jack (Ed.) *Poetry the healer*. Philadelphia: Lippincott, 1973.

Lerner, Arthur. "Poetry therapy." *American Journal of Nursing*, 1973, *73*, 1336-1338.

Pearson, Leonard (Ed.) *The use of written communications in psychotherapy*. Springfield, Ill.: Thomas, 1965.

Rothenberg, Albert. "Poetry in therapy, therapy in poetry." *The Sciences*, 1972, *12*, 30-31.

Ruesch, Jurgen. *Knowledge in action*. New York: Aronson, 1976.

Torrey, E. Fuller. *The mind game*. New York: Emerson Hall, 1972.

Vanderpool, John. "The quest for instant mental health." *Archives of General Psychiatry*, 1973, *29*, 134-137.

Van Putten, Theodore. "Milieu therapy: Contraindications." *Archives of General Psychiatry*, 1973, *29*, 640-643.

Yalom, Irvin. *The theory and practice of group psychotherapy*. New York: Basic books, 1975.

Yalom, Irvin, & Lieberman, Morton. "A study of encounter group casualties." *Archives of General Psychiatry*, 1971, *25*, 16-30.

CHAPTER 8

Action Techniques in Psychopoetry

Gilbert A. Schloss and Dominick E. Grundy

Introduction

Poetry therapy is such a new field that most of the literature at present can best be described as primarily anecdotal and testimonial. There is still much more enthusiasm than information. Some theoretical issues have been raised (Forrest, 1969; Leedy, 1973; Lerner, 1973a and b; Meerloo, 1969; Schloss, 1976) and the beginnings of research have been undertaken (Edgar & Hazley, 1969; Schloss, 1976). Little, however, has been written about poetry therapy techniques. This is not surprising, since poetry therapy is essentially an ancillary therapy approach. As a result, therapists often have simply introduced a poem within the context of their group and allowed their clients to respond. This is one way to work with poetry. There are, however, many other methods of using poetry effectively as a therapeutic tool.

To suggest our orientation, we call the particular approach to poetry therapy described in this chapter "psychopoetry." Dr. J. L. Moreno, the father of psychodrama and group psychotherapy, first used the word "psychopoetry" to refer to the introduction of poetry into the therapeutic process long before the term "poetry therapy" had been coined (see Leedy, 1969; J. L. Moreno, 1948). Reintroducing Moreno's term seems particularly appropriate since extensive use is made of psychodramatic structure, theory, and techniques.

This chapter describes and illustrates different psychopoetry techniques that have been used primarily in groups. Some are fairly well known. A few originated in the older ancillary art therapies—music, art, dance—and the various sensitivity training approaches. A large number were adapted from psychodrama. The chapter also discusses the structural patterns which emerge from psychopoetry groups. While considerable diversity exists among members of groups, there appear to be patterns within each group sufficiently similar as to fall under three headings: the psychodramatic, the sociopoetic, and the metapoetic. This division has been discussed elsewhere (Schloss, 1976) and is also treated later in this chapter.

The synthesis suggested by the term "psychopoetry" may seem unusual to those who experience drama and poetry as antithetical. Poetry is often seen as a solitary, introspective medium and drama a reflection of the social, active side of man. Historically, however, they have sources in common: Greek drama, mystery and miracle plays, Elizabethan and Jacobean theatre, and the 17th-century masque are salient examples. In our century Yeats and Eliot, among others, worked to reassociate them in poetic drama.

Psychopoetry also uses poetry in an active sense. When the poet looks into himself, translating thoughts and emotions into words and images, he creates a poetic form which is read by another. The expression of his being communicates with that of the reader, striking a responsive chord through the crystallization into words of the poet's inner experience. The reader recognizes an echo of his feelings and derives emotional impact from the poem; in turn this furthers exploration of his own emotions for which he may now acquire words, symbols, and images (Freud, 1908). Aiding his client to find words for his feelings and early experiences is an important task of the therapist, and the act of giving them verbal, especially poetic, form provides something external on which he and the client can focus together.

Here, perhaps, is a place to distinguish between the poetry judged under the standards of a work of art and that written by a client as part of the psychotherapy process he is experiencing. A client may or may not produce a work that is esthetically appealing and worth considering by others as having artistic value. The therapist, however, is not primarily concerned with the esthetics of the poem. For him, the work is a vehicle for helping the client explore himself. This exploration, not the poem itself, is paramount. The poem, then, expresses the heightened emotions of the client, whether it reflects artistic merit or not.

Techniques

Most techniques described here are primarily intended for groups. Several, however, such as spontaneous writing and the extended metaphor, could be used individually. The techniques below are considered highly effective, yet should never be applied inflexibly or without proper consideration of the circumstances of the therapeutic milieu. They may be used also in a sequence or format different from that envisaged here.

Warm-Ups

A group member who comes to a psychopoetry group may have spent his day in various ways and experienced different moods and situations: perhaps he received a raise or was fired, fought or made love with his wife, ate too much or too little. Whatever his day, he will carry some of it with him into the group. If the group he attends has not been meeting for long, he may experience some anxiety when he arrives. There are people he does not yet know. Will they respond to him and accept him? Will he be part of the group? One of the functions of the warm-up is to provide a common experience to which the group members can initially relate. The warm-up, then, acts as a bridge between the outside world and the mutual experiences of the group. It helps to break the tension of the new situation and to bring group members to the point where they feel free enough to work on themselves productively.

A common warm-up is to have a group member or leader simply read a poem and then solicit reactions. This approach may meet with little or no response, particularly when the group is new. Something more structured often has to be introduced to help the group members feel comfortable with each other. One very effective warm-up is a mix. A poem can be read which suggests an introduction, such as Emily Dickinson's "I'm nobody. Who are you?"

> *I'm nobody. Who are you?*
> *Are you nobody too?*
> *Then there's a pair of us.*
> *Don't tell—they'd banish us, you know.*
> *How dreary to be somebody,*
> *How public—like a frog—*
> *To tell your name the livelong June*
> *To an admiring bog.**

Instead of expressing their feelings or reactions directly to the whole group, members are asked to approach someone in it whom they do not know but would like to meet. They then introduce themselves, describing how they felt when the poem was read.

A variation is to have a group member tell another why he joined the group, what he hopes to get out of it, or how he feels about poetry. After allowing a few minutes for interaction, each member introduces the person he spoke to and tells the group what that person said.

By means of the mix, valuable biographical, emotional, and vocational information is often exchanged and shared with the group. Each member has now at least one other with whom he has directly interacted, either because he chose to or was chosen. He also has heard something about the other people in the group.

---

*Poem #288 reprinted by permission of the publishers and Trustees of Amherst College from THE POEMS OF EMILY DICKINSON, edited by Thomas H. Johnson, Cambridge, Mass.: The Belknap Press of Harvard University Press, Copyright © 1951, 1955 by the President and Fellows of Harvard College.

Another warm-up for a relatively new group is the creation of a group poem. One method for introducing this is to read a poem which has contrasting images, for example, Robert Frost's "Fire and Ice."

> *Some say the world will end in fire,*
> *Some say in ice.*
> *From what I've tasted of desire*
> *I hold with those who favor fire.*
> *But if it had to perish twice,*
> *I think I know enough of hate*
> *To say that for destruction ice*
> *Is also great*
> *And would suffice.** *

Members are asked which they most closely identify with at the moment—fire or ice—and the leader breaks the group into subgroups of four or five, each composed of members choosing the same image. The subgroup then collaborates on a poem related to that image. The task has a fairly short time limit, perhaps 10 or 15 minutes. A representative, selected by each subgroup, reads the poem to the larger group, and others respond to it.

This warm-up provides a task in which people interact and cooperate to achieve a common goal. It offers a vehicle for group interchange of feelings. There is also the opportunity to examine how people in the various subgroups worked with each other, how they felt toward each other, how each responded to the problem they were presented with, and what roles each saw others playing. Also, the members have shared something among themselves, the creation of a poem. Mutual authorship is often a less threatening step for an individual risking exposure than presenting one of his own poems.

In another warm-up for a new group the leader has group members sit back, relax, close their eyes, and try to get in touch with what they feel right then. After a few moments, the leader passes out sheets of paper and asks each member to write a few lines describing as directly as possible what he is feeling.

To lessen initial inhibition, the leader can suggest that each group member, if he desires, start his piece with the words "I feel." Members should be assured that no one will have to read aloud against his will. The leader can also explain that while each will be writing a poem, the total effect of all the pieces read will be a group poem expressing the feelings of the group as a whole.

Only five or six minutes should be given to the writing part of this warm-up, so that members do not have time to become self-conscious in

---

*From THE POETRY OF ROBERT FROST edited by Edward Connery Lathem. Copyright 1923, 1928, © 1969 by Holt, Rinehart and Winston. Copyright 1951 © 1956 by Robert Frost. Reprinted by permission of Holt, Rinehart and Winston, Publishers and Jonathan Cape Ltd., Publishers, and the Estate of Robert Frost.

rereading their poems and begin crossing out parts of them. Yet the leader should avoid making the exercise seem like a timed school exam. It is usually best for the leader not to ask if anyone wishes to read his piece until all have stopped writing. Often those who finished early are more likely to read immediately to put an end to the tension of waiting.

An example of the kind of poem coming out of this exercise is the following:

> *I feel lost*
> *like a very little girl*
> *in a very big place*
> *full of space,*
> *scary things*
> *and strange grown-ups.*
> *I'm scared.*

Another poem which also expresses some humor is one a client titled "Feeling."

> *When I am feeling*
> *sour*
> *I will*
> *water*
> *my plants*
> *with*
>
> *grapefruit*
> *juice.*

When the pieces are read, the leader may ask if any group members can relate their own experiences to any of the emotions expressed. Often, some of the stronger feelings in a piece are identified with by a member admitting he also had felt that way, but did not feel safe enough to explore the feeling. Especially if the group is at its beginning stages, many of the emotions are those of loneliness, being on the outside, anxiety about the group—all of which are frequent concerns when individuals have not yet made connections with other group members. These feelings often serve as an initial bond because members find they have in common this experience of not relating.

A more extensive and elaborate warm-up is usually indicated when a group is new. Once the group has been meeting for a while and relationships have begun to develop, warm-ups may become less elaborate and more spontaneous. For example, a warm-up might begin with someone mentioning something that had happened during the week. Someone else might present a poem started in a previous group and polished during the week. Another might bring in a poem he came across that touched him and that he wanted to share. A group theme could evolve from any of these spontaneous warm-ups.

Time Techniques

Many techniques described here move back and forth in time, as well as in and out of it. They can be compared with J. L. Moreno's "surplus reality," a simulated reality in which laws of "pastness" and "futurity" are abrogated, where the individual can try something out free of consequences. Movement into the past is called age regression; into the future, it is called future projection. On appropriate occasions, to gain different kinds of perspective, a client may be asked to fantasize a timeless place where responsibilities for his behavior do not exist (Z. Moreno, 1959, 1965).

As Kurt Lewin has pointed out (Lewin, 1935), man lives in the perpetual present. The past ceases to exist once it is over. What remain are those memories and feelings—unfinished business—which we carry with us and which still affect us in the present. In psychopoetry, age regression techniques reflect Lewin's concept. They are a means of exploring in the present past events with which the person is still emotionally caught up. The techniques help give these events a feeling of immediacy.

In one group, for example, several members began to speak about childhood. To facilitate their exploration, the leader suggested that they close their eyes, imagine themselves at whatever age they wished, and focus on sensual memories, such as the smells in their hallway or at school, the sounds they heard in the neighborhood, the taste of birthday cake or their favorite candy. After a few minutes, the leader asked them to open their eyes and share their memories. To make these more vivid, he instructed them to describe events in the present tense, as if they were just happening. Several members reminisced. As they did, their sentences became shorter, their words more simple. Without affecting a younger speech, they seemed to be suggesting it.

A woman began to cry. She spoke about her childhood loneliness that had been somewhat mitigated by the relationship with her mother. When she was eight her mother died. She wished she could have told her mother about feelings she had never been able to express then. The leader suggested she choose someone in the group who reminded her in any way of her mother and talk to her. The woman hesitated, then chose an older group member she had barely spoken to before. Addressing her as if she were her mother, the woman expressed sorrow, hurt, and anger because her mother died when she needed her so much.

Others also shared feelings of hurt and anger with one or both parents, or expressed tender feelings toward them which they had never revealed. The leader instructed the group members to write a poem directly addressed to the parent for whom they had these feelings. The pieces were then read and some members came into contact with feelings that had been buried for many years.

Some examples of poems coming out of this type of exercise are the following:

I'm scared
Help me.
Hold me tight.
Use no words,
And tell me—
It's all right
It's all right.
        * * *

A part of each day
my face is white
I cry
and my eyes burn
I think that I am
four
or three
I am unhappy.

Another regression technique is to focus on one element from childhood, such as a childhood game, school, the neighborhood. Finding the other introduction too diffuse, some group members may relate their experiences more easily with this structure. The leader may also ask them to image themselves as a pet, a favorite toy, or a familiar object from some time in their childhood, and to describe themselves and their family from that perspective. Since children often project their hopes, dreams, and perceptions onto toys and other objects, this technique can uncover many childhood associations.

In the future projection technique, group members explore reactions not yet taken that may help make decisions. For example, a client brought this poem into group:

The prime of my life.
This time of my life
is the prime of my life,
with a fuse and a cap and a
Panic—I can't get out—(Why do I suffer?)
Where is tomorrow?
I'll never make it (if only my life
                were in order
                in order to . . .)
Did you ever have a day
When you life turns the clock,
backwards,
        and fucks up all your growth?

Describing the context in which he wrote it, the client said he was angry with himself because he had had an opportunity for a job but threw it away. Other group members, relating to the poem, spoke of the fear they would never accomplish what they wanted to. One said that he had been thinking of taking a new job but was afraid of what would happen if he risked it. He was sure it would turn out wrong. He had been an actor and had become a salesman. Now he had the opportunity to do some theater work that meant leaving his current job.

The group leader suggested he stand up and imagine that each step he took forward would represent the passage of a month. How many would he take? The man took one step, saying he was afraid to take any more. The leader then addressed him as if it were a month later and they had just met. He asked the man what he had been doing the previous month. The group member hesitated for a moment, then responded that he was still at his sales position. He had not taken the theater work. As the leader moved him from month to month, the sketch of a life took shape in which the client moved up slowly in his firm and finally retired with a sense of his life wasted. He said he wished he had had another chance. The leader then asked him to return to the present and try again. This time the man chose the theater job, did moderately well, but had difficulty getting future work. He remained on the periphery of the theater for several years, then returned to the business world. He felt depressed at his failure. Several years later, according to his future projection, he became interested in acting and directing in community theater. He reached 65, got the same gold watch, but felt fuller. Returning once more to the present, he decided to take the theater job, saying that even though he might fail to make a career of it, he would gain experience that would allow him to keep theater as part of his life. Other group members shared feelings on the theme of taking a risk and then expressed them in writing.

The third variety of time techniques involves reflective states where the individual is placed beyond the concerns of time to evaluate his life without responsibilities. Sometimes he is led to this state as the logical extension of his future projection into death. On other occasions, he can move there when he feels numb and lethargic or even desires to die. The leader can set the stage for a death-scene fantasy. For example, the individual has just died and is interviewed by St. Peter, who attempts to find out where to send him or who he really was while alive. In another he is interviewed by the devil who offers to help him get back at those who have slighted, exploited, or hurt him. The devil suggests that the person has nothing to lose by letting out his hostile feelings since he is already in hell.

After such a scene, the leader may ask group members to write a poem expressing any feeling evoked by it. Sometimes fear of death becomes a dominant note. More often the writings focus on how, in the face of inevitable death, the group member can change his future by modifying his behavior and expressing his feelings in the present.

Another "timeless" approach involves the creation of a courtroom scene in which the group member puts on trial the significant people in his life. He decides what wrongdoings they have committed against him and the punishment they deserve for these "crimes." For example, during a group, a member read the following poem:

> *(I wonder if anybody knows I'm down here?*
> *someone's bound to come by.*
> *It may be too dark for anyone to. . . .)*
>
> *I don't understand how I can be thirty years old*
> *in a library, writing this yet*
> *I'm torn back*
> *to being Sidney on my block*
> *and the cracks on the sidewalks are for games*
> *and "it's dinner time"*
> *and afraid of my father and his belt*
> *and, "quiet, your father wants the ketchup"*
> *and when that hand gets close to the ten I'll*
> *have to go into that dark bedroom and be quiet.*
> *Go Sleep*
>
> *(At last sitting down here, it's quiet,*
> *I scrunch against these lead thick wet walls*
> *I do hope someone comes by)*
> *No! No! I didn't do it.*
> *Dad please don't. . . . Mom, I didn't*
> *do it! (Tighten Sidney as you're hit, tighten)*
>
> *(sure quiet down here, hope somebody finds me)*

The group member spoke briefly about his childhood and how he always feared the time of day when his father came home and his sins were added up. Then his mother became the prosecutor and his father the judge and jury. What made it even worse was that he, the defense attorney, was not allowed to contradict the prosecutor for fear of being punished for perjury or contempt of court.

After several group members shared their feelings about being punished as children with no real court of appeal, the leader set up a courtroom scene. The group member this time played prosecutor, judge, and jury. Stand-ins for his parents were used and he described the crime of which they were accused, presented evidence, passed judgment, and pronounced the sentence. In the course of this scene, he expressed much of the frustration and anger he could not express as a child. After releasing these feelings, he could temper his judgments and remember some good interactions with his parents. He still found them "guilty," but ended by condemning his father to become a child again and experience what he had experienced. His mother he condemned to make her own decisions rather than blindly follow his father. At the end another defendant was brought up by the leader—the group member himself—on whom he was asked to pass judgment. Suddenly he realized that he had been following his parents' path, acting as they had acted, even though he had condemned them for it. He found himself guilty as charged and sentenced himself to stop nursing childhood grievances and to concentrate on changing his own behavior in the present.

Fantasy Techniques

Fantasy techniques are effective in psychopoetry because they allow the individual to employ his imagination freely while controlling all the circumstances. As with time techniques, he can move as far away from the real as desired; he is free to essay something verbally, incorporating elements perhaps too threatening for him in reality. Fantasy often has qualities similar to those of child's play in its spontaneity and its rehearsal of rules of the adult "game" of life. Wishes and fears frequently hidden from view may be permitted to surface. Used in a group setting, the fantasy technique not only gives a dream concreteness but offers the group member the opportunity to share it with others.

Fantasy techniques are of different kinds. In one, group members are asked to imagine themselves as an object in the room and to write about life from that perspective. The choice of object and the description of its point of view are often revealing, and may provide a focus on the group member's perception of himself and his world. As a variation, he may be asked to imagine the entire group as an object of which each chooses a part; the part he chooses to become tells much about how he relates to others.

Another approach involves setting a scene and a mood but leaving the situation open-ended. For example, a person may be told that he is climbing a hill, arrives at the top, and finds a cave. Within the cave is a door; he opens the door and walks in. He is then free to fantasize what is on the other side of the door. If the mood is carefully set, he will often have a vivid experience. After his experiences have been shared, the leader can call for a writing exercise describing feelings about the scene. A variation of this fantasy is to go into a deserted house, find a trunk and look within, or find a crystal ball, gaze into it and describe what is seen.

Another fantasy technique employs a "fantasy person" with whom the individual interacts, probably played, at the leader's discretion, by another group member. Such techniques are present in the *death*, *diabolic* and *judgment* scenes described above, or in scenes called *magic shop* or *magic island* (Z. Moreno, 1959, 1965). In the latter the individual is offered a certain number of wishes that are granted, but for which payment is required. The group member may ask for general things like happiness or may have wishes related to a particular situation in his life. In either case, the person will require something in return that he does not want. Those usually include qualities he needs to discard to attain his wish. For instance, if he desires friendship with someone, he might be asked to give up anger or mistrust. The goal of the exchange is for him to explore what behavior he must give up to realize the things he wants. "Wishes" may also be made the topic for a poem by the group, and their exploration in a scene with a magic setting may then follow the reading of the poems.

Sharing

"Sharing" can be used in any group setting and in conjunction with any of the foregoing techniques. It may have an important role to play in the structure of a group, or it may be employed on a more spontaneous and occasional basis. It consists of expressing a sense of identification through narrating experiences similar to those of another group member. Comparison between problems or statements of two group members is the jumping-off point; the sharer, of course, never has an identical experience to relate. In forging an explicit link between himself and another, however, he acts supportively toward him and may also arrive at new insights himself. Emphasis is always on relating the sharer's own history rather than on judging, analyzing, or giving advice to the person shared with. The latter benefits from sharing because whatever he exposed of his life creates common ground on which he is meeting others, and he need not feel isolated by something he may have revealed (E. K. Siroka & R. W. Siroka, 1971; R. W. Siroka & E. K. Siroka, 1971).

Sharing is the concluding segment of a psychodrama; but this is not the only point at which it is used in a psychopoetry group. After a group member has reacted to a poem, other members may share with him; in turn this sharing can provide the focus of another poem. The leader may also ask members to write a poem as a response to what someone has said or to a theme suggested by it. In this case, reading back the poem is a form of sharing with the individual, and foundations are laid for new interactions between group members on the basis of their poetic responses to the theme.

Group Structure

In *Psychopoetry: A New Approach to Self-Awareness Through Poetry Therapy* (Schloss, 1976) the experiences of several hundred groups are examined. From the data, it appears that psychopoetry groups can be divided into at least three broad structural patterns: the psychodramatic, the sociopoetic, and the metapoetic. The psychodramatic pattern resembles psychodrama in that after a warm-up a protagonist emerges on whom the work of the group is centered. After he expresses his problem or concern, the group shares, as in psychodrama. The sociopoetic pattern is similar to sociodrama in that the focus is not so much on the protagonist but on a theme to which group members relate. In the metapoetic pattern, group members identify with a particular symbol or metaphor within a poem and use it to explore a problem many in the group have in common.

These patterns emerge spontaneously through the warm-up and the interaction of the group members. The key factor in determining which pattern will appear is the particular mood of the group members. A way to illustrate this is to show how on different occasions the three patterns emerged when the same poem, "Tree at My Window" by Frost was used as a warm-up.

> Tree at my window, window tree,
> My sash is lowered when night comes on;
> But let there never be curtain drawn
> Between you and me.
>
> Vague dream-head lifted out of the ground,
> And thing next most diffuse to cloud,
> Not all your light tongues talking aloud
> Could be profound.
>
> But, tree, I have seen you taken and tossed,
> And if you have seen me when I slept,
> You have seen me when I was taken and swept
> And all but lost.
>
> That day she put our heads together,
> Fate had her imagination about her,
> Your head so much concerned with outer,
> Mine with inner, weather.*

In one group, a woman responded to the reading of this poem by breaking out in tears. The poem reminded her of a tree that she would visit with her older sister. After her sister died she went there alone, particularly when upset, and spent hours sitting on a low branch against the trunk. She felt cradled and comforted there. Sometimes she said she made herself very small and pressed against the tree, as if trying to become a part of it and gain some of its strength. She sat quietly in the group for a moment, then said that after her sister died, she had no one to talk to and so would tell her troubles to the tree.

The leader moved her to the center of the group and asked her to imagine herself sitting on a branch, telling the tree her troubles. She began to cry again

---

*From the POETRY OF ROBERT FROST edited by Edward Connery Lathem. Copyright 1923, 1928, © 1969 by Holt, Rinehart and Winston. Copyright 1951 © 1956 by Robert Frost. Reprinted by permission of Holt, Rinehart and Winston, Publishers and Jonathan Cape, Ltd., Publishers, and the Estate of Robert Frost.

and, addressing the tree, talked about her recent loss of a job and the death of a friend. She said how much she missed her sister. She then addressed an auxiliary playing her sister and told her how much she loved her, a feeling she had not expressed before. She began to cry, not with the angry pain-wracked tears of the beginning, but with a quiet, softer kind of sorrow. Despite her sadness, she seemed more at peace.

In the sharing, other group members talked about their feelings of loss through death or separation. The group then was asked to write directly to a person with whom they still felt this loss. These pieces were then read. In one instance, a woman expressed missing a close childhood friend when her family moved to another city. After she read her piece, she explored feelings about that relationship. Other members shared feelings about childhood and another writing exercise occurred. Here a psychodramatic structure had emerged from the group.

In another group in which "Tree at My Window" was read, a member said he liked Frost's image of the tree concerned with outer weather and of the narrator concerned with inner weather. The member said he had not only inner weather, but a whole inner landscape of situations, events, and some personal qualities he rarely spoke about. Another member referred to a book, *The Me Nobody Knows* (Joseph, 1969), saying she had always felt like a stranger with others, even people in the group, because she had never shown who she really was. The leader suggested that members write a poem exploring "the me nobody knows" and express at least one part of themselves which they rarely showed to another. These pieces were read aloud. Some revealed childhood indiscretions. A professional man admitted that he enjoyed cooking, but felt people would laugh at him or think he was effeminate. Others shared similar experiences. Many expressed the feeling that they knew and trusted each other more than before the group began. Here a sociopoetic pattern had emerged.

In another group, after Frost's poem was read, one member wondered what it would be like to be a tree. He said he felt the tree had all the advantages, particularly in strength and solidity. The leader asked him what kind of tree he would like to be and he answered, "an oak." The leader then suggested he talk about himself as an oak. He responded that he was strong and tall, not small and weak like a human. He said that women now sought him out and stood under his branches for protection, rather than ignoring him or being unimpressed by him.

Another member chimed in with "Just wait till the dogs get through with you, pissing on your trunk, shitting on your roots, and cats scratching on your bark." He assumed the identity of a city tree planted on a street but not growing well, fighting for his life amidst the dirt, animals, and children. He felt stunted and in danger of not surviving. Later, this individual revealed that he had always wanted to live in the country and try his hand at landscape gardening. He had married young and felt trapped with a family that was constantly making demands upon him and a wife who became frightened whenever he suggested trying to change.

Other group members joined in spontaneously, became different kinds of trees and fantasized lifestyles related to the tree they chose. Often their fantasizing suggested alternate behavior, as well as revealing their problems, dreams, and desires. In the course of the group, for example, the city tree decided he was tired of being too frightened to move into the country. He felt he needed to grow strongly enough to begin to explore this alternative.

As mentioned above, the basic structure of the psychodrama is the warm-up, the drama proper, and then the sharing. Zerka Moreno (1965) describes its action as starting at the periphery and moving to the center, so that the chief concern of the protagonist is led up to gradually, not introduced prematurely before he can deal with it. In a psychodramatic psychopoetry group, a protagonist emerges from the group and explores an area; the group shares, then writes a poem related to feelings evoked by the action; members read their pieces, and then another moves to become the protagonist and the pattern is repeated. Often two, and as many as three, become protagonists in the course of the group. Unlike a psychodrama, in a psychodramatic psychopoetry group there is an ebb and flow pattern as well as a general movement from periphery to center. The ebb and flow goes from action (as a dialogue is dramatized rather than described) to reflection (the writing of a poem). After the poems are written, they are read aloud: the intensity is built up and once again released in the sharing and the writing. The movement from periphery to center, then, usually involves different protagonists. Each protagonist's flow of expression tends to be deeper and more intense than the preceding one, and each enactment represents both an exploration and a warm-up for further exploration.

While the sociopoetic pattern is like sociodrama in that it deals with a thematic concern of the whole group, the structural pattern is different. The sociopoetic group will occasionally have members representing different aspects of an emotion, such as anger or love, and then speaking from that feeling to explore the range of the emotion. More often, however, little dramatization occurs. Rather, the different group members touch upon the theme that seems to dominate the interest of the group and relate it to their personal experience.

Conclusion

There are several concepts of what poetry therapy is and how it works. Reading poetry helps break down resistance to feelings and stimulate their rise to the surface. The suggestiveness of poetry, through metaphor and imagery, communicates with primary processes. For some, the poem and the poet, too, by extension, become an understanding friend who has expressed feelings hidden in the reader and who induces a trusting response. For those whose anxiety makes communication with people difficult, writing poetry provides a safe way to confide, to say what they want to say and feel in control of the process. Some of the linguistic and artistic devices of poetry offer an indirect way of giving vent to deep feelings. In a group setting, of course, these are all supplemented by the continued interaction by which members learn to communicate, to be themselves with others, and to respond to what others reveal of themselves.

The techniques described in this chapter can be used in conjunction with different orientations to poetry therapy and, in fact, with different approaches to psychotherapy itself. A client's poem may be formally interpreted as an indirect expression of unconscious drives or as an interpersonal tool for interaction with others. These various applications are possible because poetry is readily adapted to different therapeutic orientations. Further, many of the techniques described above also have been utilized by other mental health professionals in different fields: occupational therapists, vocational therapists, social workers, and counselors are just a few.

However, a word of caution is in order. While poetry is a powerful therapeutic tool, it is only one among many. It can and has helped many, but does not help everyone. Still, its potential, particularly in relation to the dynamics of groups, has only begun to be explored.

References

Edgar, Kenneth F., & Hazley, Richard. "Validation of poetry therapy as a group therapy technique." In Jack J. Leedy (Ed.). *Poetry therapy*. Philadelphia: Lippincott, 1969. Pp. 111-123.

Forrest, David. "The patient's sense of the poem: Affinities and ambiguities." In Jack J. Leedy (Ed.), *Poetry therapy*. Philadelphia: Lippincott, 1969. Pp. 231-259.

Freud, Sigmund. "The relation of the poet to day-dreaming" (1908). In *Collected papers*, Vol. 4, edited by Ernest Jones, No. 10, pp. 173-83. New York: Basic Books, 1959.

Harrower, Molly, Crootof, Charles, Parker, Rolland, & Harari, Carmi. "Poetry as therapy and therapist as poet." *Journal of Clinical Issues in Psychology*, May 1970, *1*, 34-38.

Joseph, Stephen M. (Ed.) *The me nobody knows*. New York: Discuss Books, 1969.

Kaplan, J. "Poetry therapy." *Seventeen*, January 1973, *32*, 28.

Leedy, Jack J. (Ed.) *Poetry therapy*. Philadelphia: Lippincott, 1969.

Leedy, Jack J. (Ed.) *Poetry the healer*. Philadelphia: Lippincott, 1973.

Lerner, Arthur. "Poetry therapy." *American Journal of Nursing*, 1973a, *73*, 1336-1338.

Lerner, Arthur. "Poetry therapy: From sad to verse." *PTA Magazine*, March 1973b, *67*, 30-33.

Lewin, Kurt. *A dynamic theory of personality*. New York: McGraw-Hill, 1935.

Meerloo, Joost, A. M. "The universal language of rhythm." In Jack J. Leedy (Ed.), *Poetry therapy*. Philadelphia: Lippincott, 1969. Pp. 52-66.

Moreno, J. L. "The concept of sociodrama: A new approach to the problem of inter-cultural relations." *Sociometry*, November 1943, *6*, 434-439.

Moreno, J. L. "On the history of psychodrama." *Group Psychotherapy*, September 1958, *11*, 257-260.

Moreno, J. L. *Psychodrama*. 3 Vols. Beacon, N.Y.: Beacon House, 1946, 1948, 1969.

Moreno, J. L. *The theatre of spontaneity*. Beacon, N.Y.: Beacon House, 1947.

Moreno, J. L. *Who shall survive? Foundations of sociometry, group psychotherapy and sociodrama*. 2nd ed. Beacon, N.Y.: Beacon House, 1953.

Moreno, Zerka T. "Note on spontaneous learning 'in situ' versus learning the academic way." *Group Psychotherapy*, March 1958, *11*, 50-51.

Moreno, Zerka T. "A survey of psychodramatic techniques." *Group Psychotherapy*, March 1959, *12*, 5-14.

Moreno, Zerka T. "Psychodramatic rules, techniques and adjunctive methods." *Group Psychotherapy*, March-June 1965, *18*, 73-86.

Rance, Constance, & Price, Arlene. "Poetry as a group process." *The American Journal of Occupational Therapy*, 1973, *27*, 252-255.

Schloss, Gilbert A. *Psychopoetry: A new approach to self-awareness through poetry therapy.* New York: Grosset & Dunlap, 1976.

Schloss, Gilbert A., & Grundy, Dominick E. "Poetry therapy." *Literature and Psychology*, 1971, *21*, 51-55.

Schloss, Gilbert A., Siroka, Robert W., & Siroka, Ellen K. "Some contemporary origins of the personal growth group." In Robert W. Siroka, Ellen K. Siroka, & Gilbert A. Schloss (Eds.), *Sensitivity training and group encounter: An introduction.* New York: Grosset & Dunlap, 1971. Pp. 3-10.

Siroka, Ellen K., & Siroka, Robert W. "The psychodramatic approach to sensitivity training." In Robert W. Siroka, Ellen K. Siroka, & Gilbert A. Schloss (Eds.), *Sensitivity training and group encounter: An introduction.* New York: Grosset & Dunlap, 1971. Pp. 109-118.

Siroka, Robert W. "Psychodrama in a therapeutic community." *Group Psychotherapy*, January 1967, *20*, 123-126.

Siroka, Robert W., & Schloss, Gilbert A. "The death scene in psychodrama." *Group Psychotherapy*, December 1968, *21*, 202-205.

Siroka, Robert W., Siroka, Ellen K., & Schloss, Gilbert A. (Eds.) *Sensitivity training and group encounter: An introduction.* New York: Grosset & Dunlap, 1971.

Siroka, Robert W., & Siroka, Ellen K. "Psychodrama and the therapeutic community." In Leonard Blank, Gloria B. Gottsegen, & Monroe G. Gottsegen (Eds.), *Confrontation: Encounters in self and interpersonal awareness.* New York: Macmillan, 1971. Pp. 77-105.

CHAPTER 9

Zen Telegrams: A Warm-Up Technique for Poetry Therapy Groups

Mary Clancy and Roger Lauer

Poetry therapy is a method of treating emotional disturbances that involves listening to or creating poetry. This therapy can take place in either a one-to-one or group setting. During the past 15 years, it has been used for patients with a variety of diagnoses and has been carried out by psychiatrists, psychologists, social workers, occupational therapists, and other professionals. An extensive literature on the subject (Blanton, 1960; Curry, 1973; Greifer, 1963; Harrower, 1972; Lawler, 1972; Leedy, 1969, 1973; Lerner, 1973, 1975; Rothenberg, 1972; Ward, 1960) has generated much interest and has led to wide acknowledgment of the value of poetry therapy. Although the pioneering reports have served to legitimize this form of therapy, they have not dealt fully with some technical issues.

For example, participants in poetry therapy groups can experience difficulties in starting to write. They may feel a general inertia about moving from the world of everyday activities to the world of art, a world with different rules of perception, thinking, and behavior. They may be insecure about what they will produce or about the group's reaction to their work. They may be inhibited by a fear of exposure, ridicule, reproach, criticism, or embarrassment. They may be inhibited by a belief that they are untalented, uneducated, or inadequate.

In one of our newly formed poetry therapy groups, members were especially unwilling to write and expressed their feelings vociferously. They decided that the only subject worth addressing was "Why I don't like to write?" Their words covered a range of different fears and concerns. Here is what a 32-year-old secretary wrote:

> It's not that I don't like to write
> but when I do write something

I'm very involved in it
It's an extension of myself

The thought of subjecting my work
to scrutiny by others
sometimes makes me uneasy
I feel vulnerable

Once something has been written
It has to stand alone
unable to adapt to its own defense
yet still a part of the writer

Nevertheless, if group members can be induced to press ahead and write, they tend to enjoy the experience and relax. Their artistry pleases them and does not entail any of the dreaded consequences. They overcome their initial feelings of discomfort and awkwardness.

How then can group members quickly be put at ease and motivated to write? Over the past six years, one warm-up technique, Zen telegrams, was used with more than 200 psychiatric patients and was found to be highly effective. The patients ranged in age from 17 to 20 and carried an assortment of diagnoses, including schizophrenia and depression. Groups met weekly in day centers and inpatient wards for one to two hours and contained about five to ten patients. (For more information about these groups, see Goldfield & Lauer, 1971; Lauer, 1972; and Lauer & Goldfield, 1970.)

The term "Zen telegrams" was first used to describe free-form designs that were combined with words (Reps, 1959). These picture-poems were considered to be Zen in the sense of providing a flash of illumination. A group member brought the book that contained the telegrams to a group session and suggested they be used. The results were stimulating and productive.

To create Zen telegrams in a therapy group, the following facilities and equipment are needed:

1. A quiet setting where people are protected from interruptions and distractions. It could be a dining room, an occupational therapy room, an activities room, or a library as long as it is comfortable and cheerful.
2. Chairs and a table. A large table accommodating all participants furthers group interaction and is preferable to several small tables. The table surface can be protected with a layer of newspaper.
3. A large stack of 8 x 11 paper. Newsprint will do.
4. Paintbrushes, preferably the Japanese variety that come to a point, and India Ink—one bottle of black ink and at least five bottles containing strong colors. The brushes and the ink lend themselves to quick, spontaneous use and free-flowing drawings which evoke the

Orient. Other inks, paints, pens, pencils, or crayons are not recommended.

5. Writing instruments. If possible, the group should use brushes since they make handwriting look exotic and artistic. However, pens or pencils should be available in case some participants prefer to use them.

To begin the exercise, the leader states that the Zen telegrams are for the purpose of experimenting with words and patterns. He makes it clear that the activity will be merely a matter of following some simple instructions and that no previous experience in writing poetry or prose is necessary. The goal is for people to be spontaneous and to express what they feel. Productions are not to be judged in terms of right and wrong, good and bad, or any academic standard. The exercise is not a lesson in art or composition but rather an effort to use words and drawings to express oneself. Through his own enthusiasm, the leader seeks to generate a spirit of camaraderie, the feeling that people are working together on a common project. One ground rule is stipulated: everyone will participate fully, including the leader and staff members. Such a rule is necessary because group members readily project negative judgment about their efforts onto nonparticipating observers. They believe that mere observers are amused or contemptuous and are silently evaluating their work as "no good," "silly," or "crazy." Consequently, the patients become very self-conscious and inhibited.

Following the preliminary orientation, the group members saturate their brushes with ink. Then they are instructed to hold the brush over the upper half of the sheet of paper, close their eyes, and move their arms rapidly so as to make a design on the paper. When the group members finish drawing, they are told to open their eyes and write quickly whatever words pop into their heads. People find this portion of the exercise easy and enjoyable. After they inspect their own creation, the members generally become interested in seeing what others have done and want to share their Zen telegrams with the group. The leader may act as a role model and start first, holding up his work for display or passing it around and then reading aloud what he has written. The other group members can then follow suit. Frequently, there is laughter, delight, and discussion. Group members are encouraged to react empathically to the Zen telegrams and to describe their images and feelings. One person might swell with pride over his product and announce that this was the first creative work done since school days. Another might comment that one of the Zen telegrams reminded him of his uncle's farm and the good times he used to have there. Still another might muse that his Zen telegram related to problems that had arisen at work.

The tone in the group usually becomes more relaxed following the completion of a Zen telegram exercise. People are reassured that they have the ability to write and that exercising this ability can not only be safe but fun. Sometimes the warm-up is repeated and a special twist added. The telegram might be drawn with eyes open and with a choice of color. Alternatively, it might be drawn with one person making a design, then passing it to the next person to complete in a second color and write the accompanying text. The latter procedure stimulates group interaction.

Next, the leader may suggest reviewing the Zen telegram for a common theme or particularly intriguing idea. Then the group is asked to write further on whatever emerges. The rest of the session can be conducted according to the leader's style and philosophy of poetry therapy.

In conclusion, Zen telegrams help reduce the inhibitions of poetry therapy participants and set a tone of artistic productiveness. Zen telegrams also provide a warm-up technique that ranks high in terms of several criteria. It involves equipment that can readily be obtained and utilized. It is easy for the leader to organize and for the participant to carry out. It is usable in a variety of settings and situations. It can be done quickly and is well-accepted by group members.

Examples of Zen Telegrams

an encounter

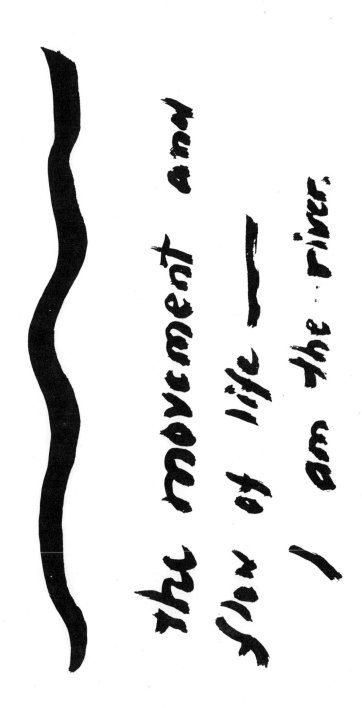

the movement and flow of life — I am the river.

The mountains
back away
in fear

TREE WITH
Gentle Blossoms

References

Blanton, Smiley. *The healing power of poetry*. New York: Crowell, 1960.

Curry, A. *Bring forth forms*. Paradise, Calif.: Dust Books, 1973.

Goldfield, Michael, & Lauer, Roger. "The use of creative writing in young adult drug abusers." *The New Physician*, 1971, *20*, 449-457.

Greifer, Eli. *Principles of poetry therapy*. New York: Poetry Therapy Center, 1963.

Harrower, Molly. *The therapy of poetry*. Springfield, Ill.: Thomas, 1972.

Lauer, Roger. "Creative writing as a therapeutic tool." *Hospital and Community Psychiatry*, 1972, *23*, 55-56.

Lauer, Roger, & Goldfield, Michael. "Creative writing in group therapy." *Psychotherapy: Theory, Research, and Practice*, 1970, 7, 248-252.

Lawler, Justus G. "Poetry therapy?" *Psychiatry*, 1972, *35*, 227-237.

Leedy, Jack (Ed.) *Poetry therapy*. Philadelphia: Lippincott, 1969.

Leedy, Jack (Ed.) *Poetry the healer*. Philadelphia: Lippincott, 1973.

Lerner, Arthur. "Poetry therapy." *American Journal of Nursing*, 1973, *73*, 1336-1338.

Lerner, Arthur. "Poetry as therapy." *APA Monitor*, 1975, *6*, 4.

Reps, P. *Zen telegrams*. Rutland, Vt.: Tuttle, 1959.

Rothenberg, Albert. "Poetry in therapy, therapy in poetry." *The Sciences*, 1972, *12*, 30-31.

Ward A. *Seasons of the soul*. Richmond, Va.: Knox, 1960.

CHAPTER 10

The Paraprofessional and Poetry Therapy

Louise Davis

Poetry therapy is a unique tool requiring specialized training and experience. Certainly, an essential function of the paraprofessional in poetry therapy is using poetry as a means of growth for himself as well as the patient. My purpose, therefore, is to show the function of the paraprofessional in poetry therapy.

Critical Considerations

The basic skills for working with a patient in the human services field are not much different for the paraprofessional than for the professional. Most important is the ability to listen carefully and understand well enough to help the patient gain insight into what has been said (Fleming, 1967). The paraprofessional also needs some of those qualities essential for any critical communication—namely, empathy, warmth, and honesty.

Another important aspect of training is the ability to establish psychological safety in a relationship so that patient and worker are able to share experiences without feeling threatened. A training program must, therefore, involve didactic aspects as part of the learning process plus experiential training which deals with attitudes and personal relationships.

Arnold Beisser (1971) notes that the group process offers a way to identify with the group and experience uniqueness as a person. At the same time, such an experience provides opportunity for the teacher or group leader to teach the fundamentals of group dynamics. He can point out what is going on in terms of personal adjustments taking place in the members of the group with reference to such things as manipulative techniques, nonverbal behavior, games, defensiveness, risk-taking, and personal growth.

My own experience has been that the ongoing group provides a way to combine the didactic and experiential aspects of teaching in what is probably the most effective and valuable way to learn for the paraprofessional. The group process encourages a self-paced learning that is quicker than individualized learning and more empathic and far-reaching in its effects.

Dr. Irving Berger (1969) suggests that it is nearly impossible to deal with the emotional aspects of a group when it is short term. He indicates that specific goals need to be kept in mind and that it is important to know when the concern is with anxieties about the role of student or therapist as against disturbances of ego function. The solution of the problem, then, probably comes in defining the contract between the leader and the group members. Part of the individual development of the student therapist is the development of sensitivity and awareness of feelings, attitudes, and internal dynamics. In a training group, the basic goal is to develop the skills of a helping person. Contributing to that goal is the gaining of insight into difficulties the group member may have in personal functioning. This insight also contributes to the development of the therapist as a helping person.

With groups operating from a nonhumanistic orientation, there is a much wider gap between a training group and a therapeutic group. In a psychodynamic group, for example, problems are viewed within the medical model as signs of psychological dysfunction. Therapy is seen as "treatment process." The leader of the group tends to give interpretations with the goal of gaining insight into underlying causes of specific disturbances. The difference in the contract has more meaning when the leader is operating from a psychodynamic group orientation. The leader's functioning, from this viewpoint, would tend to relate interpretations to the understanding of individual psychodynamics.

If a group has been defined as a training group, the goal of which is increasing understanding of the principles of human behavior or functioning, such behavior on the part of the group leader could be inappropriate and threatening. It would seem evident that the training of the paraprofessional will at some point involve what can be termed personal therapy or counseling for the paraprofessional.

Another issue which appears in training is the delineation of the terms of the relationship between the paraprofessional and professional function. Professionals themselves seem to disagree on exactly how the paraprofessional function is to be defined. Salvador Minuchin (1969) speaks of the problems as being more apparent in agencies where the medical model predominates as opposed to community health organizations developed in the community by people who live and work there. Where this medical model prevails, the professional sees the paraprofessional as a real threat, since the paraprofessional does not have the qualifications to "cure" anyone. Minuchin notes that the lack of a diploma, rather than the paraprofessional's ability to work in the field, is the deciding factor in job placement. Minuchin indicates, however, that in community organized centers the paraprofessional has more opportunity to be accepted. But Minuchin does recommend adequate training for the paraprofessional and also believes that the patient should be seen as part of his environment, rather than separate, as the medical model would imply.

Margaret Rioch notes that some of the NIMH instructors question the need for the paraprofessional in the mental health field (1963, p. 688). However, Dr. Francine Sobey (1970, p. 97), writing specifically about the use of the paraprofessional in NIMH projects, states that paraprofessionals work in areas not previously explored by the professional. Sobey indicates that the team treatment approach where disciplinary barriers are ignored is a valid approach, an approach in which each person responding has skills which can be used. As against the diploma on the wall being the deciding factor of who treats whom, Sobey advocates using available human resources as a more effective way of treating people in addition to providing them with faster service. She notes that, statistically, it is almost impossible for everyone who needs professional help to obtain it. There are simply not enough professionals available. Additionally, not everyone has the means to pay for professional help. Sobey also sees that the development of a relationship between the paraprofessional and the client is important and that this relationship and the educational value it involves will probably outweigh the medical model.

Our way of handling problems in the program at Woodview-Calabasas Hospital is to have a meeting after each group session. We discuss how we have seen the group process, theorize how we might have handled any particular problem, and receive comments from the supervising psychologist or social worker on what he has observed. In addition, we meet once a week with Dr. Lerner in a poetry therapy group. Many of us write our own poetry and we bring poetry to share and work on. At times, our therapy sessions become a poetry workshop in which we explore different ways of writing a poem and of saying more clearly what we have already said. All of us have been or are presently involved in therapy. We have learned that many of our problems are dissolved in working together. The professional learns his limits as does the paraprofessional. The relationship becomes complementary rather than one of confrontation.

The methods I have been discussing (didactic information plus experiential knowledge, therapy plus education) along with necessary personal qualities, all suggest that a viable training program needs to be flexible. For example, in poetry therapy, paraprofessionals are employed in school settings, counseling centers, hospitals, geriatric centers, and private and public mental health clinics, all of which have their own schedules and special procedures. Certainly, these various work situations must be considered in organizing a training program for paraprofessionals.

My Experience as a Paraprofessional

Poetry therapy is a way of getting in touch with others and with oneself. In my personal therapy, poetry writing was my way of getting in touch with myself. I know that reading and writing poetry is a way of sharing good and bad feelings in which the poem becomes a third party in the transaction.

Our sessions at Woodview-Calabasas Hospital began with one session a week. Within a few months we were having two weekly sessions. These sessions became more formalized as we learned what worked for us. We found that starting with what we termed a warm-up, a reading of two to four lines of poetry, we sometimes triggered responses faster than with longer poems. We also learned that coming prepared with a particular topic in mind (such as love or hate or anger) and reading pertinent poems expedited the therapeutic process.

Working with a patient in poetry therapy, we often refer back to lines we have already read. Many times a patient will feel threatened by something said or done. We may then turn our attention to another line or even to another poem that says what we are trying to convey to the patient in a different way. The poem may have been written hundreds or even thousands of years ago, yet express exactly what we are discussing, for example, "Better is a handful with quietness than both hands full with travail and vexation of spirit" *Ecclesiastes*, 4-6, and, again from *Ecclesiastes*, 9-11, where the poet clarifies creatively:

> I returned, and saw under the sun that the race is not to the swift, nor the battle to the strong, neither yet bread to the wise, nor yet riches to men of understanding, nor yet favor to men of skill; but time and chance happeneth to them all.

Through the poet's perspective, then, the patient may experience reality in a new and different way by being offered an alternative choice, one which was not apparent earlier.

Sometimes we may listen to a poem written by the patient in which he struggles to express himself, his feelings about his world, or his feelings about himself. Again the poem can be used in a noncritical way to check out where the patient was or is at this moment. In dealing with his emotions through his own or another's poetry, he has a chance to stand back and look at himself from another viewpoint because once the poem is written it stands separate and clear. The patient may then recognize more clearly his own responsibility for where he is. At the same time, we can work to find a way in which he is comfortable with himself and his feelings about himself. Eventually, he may begin to see some similarity in how he responds to others and how others respond to him.

Poetry therapy, as an adjunct to more formal psychotherapy, offers a therapeutic modality that has as one of its main features a possibly less threatening effect than formal psychotherapy. Many of our patients have talked of how the group is more like a lecture-discussion class than therapy. They have mentioned that they dislike being challenged in the direct manner that occurs in group therapy. One patient said, "Poetry therapy is like group therapy, only kinder."

Creative writing in the form of a poem or simple prose lines is often used in our groups at Woodview-Calabasas Hospital. Considering the poem and examining more concretely what it says about the patient in terms of his desires, needs, and feelings enables us to use the poem as a projective technique. To say to a patient, "Write me a poem," allows the patient to reveal himself without getting caught up in his fears of revealing himself. The poem acts in an indirect way to stimulate his ability to understand himself. Time and again I have seen a patient grow imaginatively and positively by writing about his feelings in poetry.

Sometimes the patient is afraid of seeming foolish if he writes poetically. When patients are encouraged to write and begin to risk exposing themselves, they often begin by being observers of themselves. Later, they write in terms of "I," moving in an almost regular pattern from the objective to the subjective. In so doing, they come to terms with their alienation. For some, it is the first time they have done anything creative, something that is truly their own. Lauer and Goldfield (1970) note that such writing helped patients become more self-aware. And because patients thereby felt better about themselves, group sessions became more effective.

In our groups we have tended to structure the writing around the group session, although at times we have used pre-selected topics. Ordinarily, the writing is done at the halfway point. Then we all share what has been written. If patients do not desire to share what they have written, we simply state that perhaps they will be willing to share next time and usually they do. Like Lauer and Goldfield, we have sometimes selected a simple phrase, "If I were invisible," and asked for the patient's reaction in two to four lines. Some have been unwilling to write, but most have enjoyed the chance to fantasize how they would be if they were something or someone else. One substantial gain is the increased value the "writer" places on himself when he finds he can truly state his feelings and share them with others. Finally, we may conclude that when people read or write poetry, they tap a creative, spiritual force which enables them to use the metaphoric content of their own lives to explore and find alternative solutions to their problems.

References

Beisser, Arnold R. "Identity formation within groups." *Journal of Humanistic Psychology*, 1971, *2*, 139.

Berger, Irving L. "Resistances to the learning process in group dynamics programs." *The American Journal of Psychiatry*, 1969, *126*, 851.

Fleming, John. "Teaching the basic skills of psychotherapy." *Archives of General Psychiatry*, 1967, *16*, 416.

Lauer, Roger, & Goldfield, Michael. "Creative writing in group therapy." *Psychotherapy: Theory, Research, and Practice*, 1970, *7*, 248-252.

Minuchin, Salvador. "The paraprofessional and the use of confrontation in the mental health field." *American Journal of Orthopsychiatry*, 1969, *39*, 727.

Rioch, Margaret J., Elkes, Charmian, Flint, Arden A., Usdansky, Blanche Sweet, Newman, Ruth G., & Silber, Earle. "National Institute of Mental Health pilot study in training mental health counselors." *American Journal of Orthopsychiatry*, July 1963, *33*, 682-83.

Sobey, Francine. *Nonprofessional revolution in mental health*. New York: Columbia University Press, 1970.

CHAPTER 11

Practical Considerations of Bibliotherapy

Julius Griffin

Introduction

Writers in classical Greece were well aware of the therapeutic effects of reading. Aristotle believed that literature, as well as the other arts, aroused emotions which had healing effects. The library at Thebes bore the inscription, "The Healing Place of the Sane." A similar inscription, "The Medicine Chest for the Soul," is found in the medieval Abbey Library of St. Gall, in Switzerland.

However, the mere exposure of a person to books or other forms of literature is not necessarily bibliotherapeutic. In my own efforts to understand people's emotional problems and relieve them of their stresses, I have learned to define and use bibliotherapy as "the scientific application of literature toward a therapeutic goal." A bibliotherapeutic experience, then, is more than just a reading experience because it involves the treatment of emotional problems under the guidance of a trained therapist.

To highlight the importance of understanding emotionally disturbed patients as human beings, let us reflect on the difference between a jail and a therapeutic community. In jail we incarcerate people who were judged to have hurt or offended society, and who generally are considered not able to deal appropriately with the everyday realities of life as defined by the society in which they live. In a psychiatric therapeutic community we may have some people who have hurt society and many who are not able to deal adequately with life's demands. In most jails when a prisoner displays anger, he is punished by a direct retaliation of anger, such as physical punishment or solitary confinement. In a psychiatric therapeutic community, the essential difference is that when somebody expresses anger, either verbally or by overt action, we do not retaliate with anger. We restrain him with a therapeutic goal in mind.

114

Our understanding deviant behavior is, therefore, the key to meaningful alteration of disturbed feelings and thinking into healthy adjustments. Only when we learn to understand deviant behavior can we recommend healthier alternatives so that all of us can maintain more satisfactory relationships with each other. It is this one principle which will allow therapeutic success as opposed to the old-style incarceration or custodial care.

In the above comparison of jails and therapeutic communities, I use the word "jail" advisedly because a jail might be disguised in the form of a mental hospital. In fact, some mental hospitals have been or are worse than jails. Fortunately, in many parts of the world there is now a continuing effort to eliminate the custodial concept and replace it with a therapeutic one.

Some Characteristics of Mental Illness Considered Amenable to Relief by Bibliotherapy Techniques

Many psychiatric patients have an outstanding pathological symptom—they have not been able to deal with reality in a way that is comfortable for them and/or society. One of our primary goals is to help patients deal with reality more constructively so that they can tolerate society better and society can tolerate them.

Another outstanding characteristic of mental illness is fear. Fear takes many forms and is sometimes expressed in strange ways. In our therapeutic effort, we bring frightened people into a sheltered, structured environment where we say to them, "We will attempt to help you control yourself since you have demonstrated an inability or a reduced ability to use judgment and experience and common sense in dealing with the world." Many patients become so frightened that they retreat from "our world." Our job is to bring them back. Many patients say either verbally or through their actions, "Prove to me that the world of reality is better than 'my world' . . . (my crazy world) . . . Why should I come out of my retreat? Out there (in your world, in the world of reality) I've got to work. Out there, people are frightening; out there people don't understand me. Out there, people chastise me; people hit me; people hurt me; people desert me. Why should I go out?"

Emotionally sick people are generally afraid of what their feelings or other people's feelings have done to them. They have to be reassured that it is not inevitably dangerous to experience their feelings. Most, if not all, people who are mentally ill are frightened. If we can reduce the fright in our patients, we have come a long way. Literature can help patients become less confused, less frightened, and thereby we may guide them to an understanding of their feelings. From that understanding, we hope to encourage them to experience, to trust, and to use their feelings as they cope with the vicissitudes of life.

How literature helps an emotionally disturbed person is a complex phenomenon, not yet clearly understood or scientifically validated. But my own efforts for 25 years lead me to the clinical belief that literature can and does help some persons gain or regain a healthy homeostasis. Any behavior which renders a person persistently tense, dissatisfied, incompetent, or ineffectual may be described as disturbed or pathological. When a person is unable to live a satisfying, productive life in harmony with himself and others, we say that he is emotionally disturbed. What specifically causes an individual to become mentally ill is still a matter of conjecture, even to experts, and is the subject of continued research.

However, we do have ample evidence that what a person expects of himself and of others is crucial in the etiology of mental illness. If someone sees people in an unrealistic way, or if he has an inaccurate, distorted, or fuzzy view of himself, he may be unable to deal effectively with the world. We must strive to help the disturbed person correct his distortions, misrepresentations, or unreal expectations so he can be helped to experience the world as it really is. Literature, then, can be a reality-correcting experience in which the disturbed person can see how other people see themselves, their situations, and their world. Through literature, the disturbed person can experience consensual validation. When he comes to realize that his own emotions and reactions are very similar to characters in a story, many of his feelings and thoughts often lose their frightening quality. As a result, the disturbed person may lose his sense of isolation and learn that he too is human, that to be human is to have problems, and that what is important is not just having problems but what we do with them.

Professional Responsibilities of a Bibliotherapist

Patients may see only one meaning in a certain story. The bibliotherapist must be aware of the patient's difficulties and needs. The bibliotherapist has to study and understand the patient so as to help him see that there may be two or more meanings in the story being read. If the therapist is successful, then the patient's perceptual receptivity is increased. If this enlargement of a patient's viewing can be obtained with a simplistic story, an even more expanded view could be hoped for with the use of a more complex form. For example, when the patient stumbles and says, "But, Doctor, I don't understand that sentence," I say, "Let's talk about it. Let's see if we can help you understand it." With responses from the patient, we can then talk, and this communication and mutual examination of a task is an avenue for further exploration and growth.

I enjoy reading Dr. Seuss' books to children, books such as, *The Cat in the Hat* and *Yertle the Turtle*. When I was a psychiatric consultant to a Catholic orphanage, I would read stories to several groups of young girls, four to seven years old. I did more than just read. We talked, we formed groups, and we discussed the morals and concepts in Dr. Seuss' books. *Yertle the Turtle* is a trilogy including *Gertrude McFuzz*, and *The Big Brag*. *The Big Brag* is a story of a rabbit who claims he is the best in the world because he can hear a fly nine miles away. The bear says he can smell two hummingbirds' eggs in a pond 50 miles away, and the one on the left is a little stale. A worm listens to these two braggarts and says, "I can see better than both of you." He stares ahead for a half hour and finally he says, "Well, I've seen around the world right back to this hill and I see the two biggest darn fools that ever lived."

Can you imagine how I used this story psychotherapeutically and bibliotherapeutically with four- to seven-year-old girls? Try to imagine how I would have used *Gertrude McFuzz* bibliotherapeutically.

> Gertrude was a little girl bird who had only one little plain tail feather, but she wanted two, like Lollie Le Loo. She ate a magic pill and suddenly had two tail feathers. So she ate another magic pill and she had three; she ate all thirty-six pills that were growing on the pillberry vine, and eventually she got so many feathers that she couldn't fly. Finally, they had to pluck out the extra feathers one by one; she was wiser because the one little tail feather now suited her just fine.*

Imagine how I might use this story in helping little girls who come from disturbed homes develop a healthy perspective in terms of the values of life, and of self-image.

Are There Pitfalls in Bibliotherapy?

The question is sometimes asked whether there can be harm in the indiscriminate use of literature. I must answer "yes," but in elaboration, I wish to point out that there can be potential harm in the indiscriminate use of almost anything. In its place, hugging a girl is fine, but the indiscriminate use of hugging can be harmful. The indiscriminate use of aspirin can be detrimental. In fact, the indiscriminate use of something we think is "therapeutic"—psychotherapy—can be detrimental.

For instance, giving *Don Quixote* to a psychotic patient who deals unrealistically with the world might be foolish. It might be an indiscriminate prescription. You will recall that Don Quixote was a total failure in the real world in which he lived and developed the fantasy that he was a knight. However, even after he imagined himself to be a heroic knight, he was not able to use the real world as it existed, and so he imagined that the windmills were dragons and that he fought the windmills. In a bibliotherapeutic discussion of *Don Quixote*, the harm to our patient would be if we agreed with him that the make-believe world of Don Quixote was reality. I remind you that our goal is to help the patient see that living the world of reality can be better than hiding in

---

*Adapted from Theodor Seuss Geisel (Dr. Seuss), YERTLE THE TURTLE AND OTHER STORIES. New York: Random House, 1958.

his fantasy world. The patient could say, "But Don Quixote found pleasure in his fantasy." The psychotherapeutic task would then lead to a closer examination of judgment, perception, alternative choices, ability to appraise, and eventually to consolidating all these into a workable matrix of living.

People who are mentally sick are often not judicious in their perception; they are disturbed in how they see the world. Mentally ill people "need to see things" in a way that they hope will make them more comfortable. Often, their distortions do not prove to be comfort producing, and at this point the task of the mental health professional begins.

Prescribing a specific type of literature depends, therefore, upon the needs and capacities of the individual patient. For the "chronic ward type" of hospitalized patient who doesn't communicate, I have found that *Reader's Digest* is often a good starter because it's "safer." Generally, the articles in *Reader's Digest* are short, happy, noncontroversial, informative, and interesting. Another reason for selecting *Reader's Digest* is that the patient can read about "familiar places" he can locate on a map.

Sometimes I get a globe of the earth and if we talk about France, the patient can put his finger on that spot on the globe. Although a globe isn't the actual world, it is a tangible and fairly accurate representation. People sometimes questionably comment, "Suppose a patient just takes a book and thumbs through the pages and hasn't seen anything in it and hands it back to you?" My reply is, "How do we know he hasn't seen anything in it? Can we be sure he was unseeing?" But let us assume for discussion's sake he *doesn't* see anything. The fact is he handed it back to me! Sometimes I've worked for months to get somebody to hand something back to me. He handed it back. He was the giver and I the receiver. The receiver is a real person; there is a relationship between us. We also want the giver to feel like a real person. This is the first part of significant communication and the first step in the journey of the thousand miles from mental illness to mental health.

Another question indicative of people's lack of knowledge or apprehension of therapy techniques is, "Can the group hurt a patient?" Yes, the group can "hurt" a patient. Several patients who were threatened by the sexual talk of another patient dropped out of the group and became overtly disturbed. Other patients, when called upon repeatedly to join in a discussion, could not speak and felt obliged to drop out. Several patients who were in the original group transferred at their own request to the group that met during the daytime. You can "hurt" patients, but my philosophy is this: If such a situation, if such a condition, if such an interaction "hurts" a patient and makes him regress, this is a valuable index as to his ego capacity and functioning capability. If this interaction is going to hurt him, what will be the threat of a job to his hold on reality? The threat of a week-end pass? The threat of a family visit? If in this protective bibliotherapy group situation, patients are going to regress, then we should utilize this regression as part of their therapeutic regimen.

An Experience in Setting Up
Patient Literary Discussion Groups
in a Psychiatric Hospital

During my psychiatric residency in a Veterans' Administration hospital, I had an ambulatory "catatonic" schizophrenic patient who hadn't spoken in several years. Many people had tried unsuccessfully to help this man. I had also tried and failed. One day in the library, the librarian approached this apparently muted patient and the patient responded verbally. I immediately ventured to use the librarian as my therapeutic wedge. I became aware that a book in the hospital library had been a means of relating between a librarian and a patient, and in exchange the patient apparently felt secure.

It may have been the librarian could have handed the patient an ice cream cone and the response might have been the same. The patient may not have been responding to the book but to the perfume the librarian was wearing, or to her reaching out to him as one human being to another. But somehow it made sense to me that the librarian in a library handed the patient a book and he responded. I excitedly and naively thought that this exchange was "bibliotherapy." The librarian "used" a book to do "therapy."

I must say that I have since become more conservative in my definition of bibliotherapy, and I am now disinclined to say that bibliotherapy simply involves books and a patient's getting better. I would like to emphasize once again that bibliotherapy is not merely the use of a book given to a patient by somebody. For me, it seems necessary and worthwhile to define bibliotherapy as I have in my opening statement, "the scientific application of literature toward a therapeutic goal."

For a starter, then, I approached the librarian and asked whether she thought that patients could be helped by books or literature. We asked ourselves, "What is it we want?" What is it we expect out of a bibliotherapy project? As a psychiatrist I said, "I want my patients to get better." The librarian said, "I want to be able to use the library and all its books to help your patients get better." After closer examination, we realized that neither of us really knew a whole lot about whether literature helps people get well, and if it does how it does.

We decided to ask a research psychologist for advice on how to approach the problem scientifically. We said, "We want to help patients get well, and if possible, use literature in addition to all other modalities that are used." After an initial search of the archives, the librarian reported that most of the literature dealt with the librarians' laments that doctors weren't interested. We went back to the literature again and perused it for "bibliotherapy" over the previous 50 years. We became convinced that there really had not been any prolonged scientific approach to the understanding and utilization of bibliotherapy. We became acutely aware that most psychiatrists while they did not deride bibliotherapy, just weren't knowledgeable or interested. In discussing this apathy with my colleagues, I had the feeling that their lack of interest was due to their lack of awareness of what literature could do.

The librarian and I continued to heed the advice of the research psychologist with respect to recording our efforts. Therefore, from the beginning, the librarian and I exchanged notes, ideas, and thoughts *on paper*. In addition, we would talk to each other when we met each other in the hall or when we met informally over coffee.

In due time, we decided to form a patients' "literary discussion group." At that time, I was the psychiatrist-physician on a closed ward for women. I knew that one particular patient was interested in literature because about a month earlier she had requested my administrative approval to spend $20.00 of her money for a correspondence course in American literature. She happened to be a schizophrenic patient who was in the process of returning to the world of reality. In recalling her interest in literature, I thought she would form a good nucleus for our group. When I asked if she would be interested in joining the librarian and me in a project talking about books, she said "Wonderful!"

The librarian knew many of the patients in the hospital and was familiar with those who read a lot and used the patients' library. We decided to invite five other women patients to join us. I approached these women first because they were on my ward. All five said, "Yes, I would like to be involved in discussing books." Then I said, "The librarian will come in and talk to you and tell you a little more about the plan." After the librarian and I had approached each patient individually, we went back together to personally invite them at a specific time and place to join us in the first meeting. I emphasize this procedure because it demonstrates how we reached out to the patients.

I reached out as their doctor, their ward physician, their psychiatrist, their authority figure. I invited and they responded to me. The librarian—the woman, the mother figure, the lady-friend, the person to whom they could go for literary information—also approached these people individually so that they could express, without my being present, any objection, fright, or fear that they might have of me or of the new experience. Then, when these people were receptive to the librarian as well as to me, we approached them together. Thus, the librarian and I were recognized as the co-leaders, the co-therapists, the people to whom the patients could look for advice, support, strength, and guidance in this new interpersonal excursion made on the magic carpet of literature.

Thus, for our literary project, we deliberately chose to meet at 6:30 P.M. in the patients' library. We chose 6:30 P.M. because this allowed time for the librarian and me to eat dinner and time for me to go home and change into civilian clothes. (At the hospital, the doctors and staff regularly wore white uniforms.) Moreover, 6:30 P.M. did not interfere with the patients' mealtime and gave them an equal opportunity to dress up. At our hospital, there were no uniforms of any kind for the women patients, although the men wore green pants or pajamas except when they went on pass. I arranged for the women to wear any of the dressy clothes that they had in the clothing storage room. This was one of the initial successful qualities of our approach: *We thought of them as women!* We were just as much interested in their appearance, self-image, and self-esteem as their interest in literature.

Why did we choose the patients' library? In a practical sense, it was the only private place in the hospital available to us at night. We did not want to use the ward dayroom because we wanted to make this a unique and private experience. We allowed all these patients to come to the library by themselves; they were not escorted by an aide or by me. I took a chance here because although four of these patients had "open privileges," two of the women had not been off the ward in three years without an attendant.

What I did in regard to the group members was to suggest that all six patients come together. Thus, if the two ran, strayed, or got confused, the other four would help. At no time in the two years that I was active in the group did any patient abuse the privilege or fail in going to or returning from the meeting without attendants.

The library we used was typical of most patients' libraries in an outdated, overcrowded Veterans' Administration hospital of the 1950s—a converted barrack-style, emergency, temporary erection of the World War II turmoil. We wondered how we should meet and greet the group members. The outer library door, which was ordinarily closed at that time of night, was left ajar, and we placed a sign immediately adjacent to it: "Special Meeting by Invitation Only—Patients' Bibliotherapy Group in Session." We gave recognition that something unique was going on. The door was open so that the invited patients did not have to knock. This meant that they could feel free to enter because they were part of the group. We anticipated that when the patients arrived, we would greet them by name, "Hi, Miss Jones," or "Hello, Mrs. Smith."

The librarian and I acted as hostess and host for that first meeting. We were "welcoming the patients to an interchange experience." On the desk near the entrance, we had previously arranged name cards with the first and last names of the patients, Miss Selma Jones, Mrs. Susie Smith. I was wearing my name card, "Dr. Julius Griffin," and the librarian was also wearing hers. Because of my personal preference, I do not let patients call me by my first name, and the librarian likewise seldom, if ever, allowed patients to call her by her first name. We invited the members to take their name cards. We did not offer to put it on them, but if they needed assistance the librarian helped them. To minimize any "sexual threats" to the patient, I did not touch the body of the women, and I did this by avoiding the task of pinning the name tag on their blouse or dress.

We had previously arranged the chairs in a circle. At first, I moved the chairs before and after the meeting. Later on, the janitor did the moving; still later, the male members of our group (added to the original all-woman core) came in early and stayed after the meeting to perform this task. Ash trays were strategically located. Off to one side, I had previously arranged a blackboard. Over in another corner, the librarian had arranged ten bottles of soft drinks, paper cups and napkins. We provided for an extra supply of refreshments in case someone wanted second helpings.

When all the name tags were affixed, we invited the patients to sit down. I took the initiative and started by saying, "We are going to try to have fun with literature; this is our goal." I went on briefly to describe what we would expect of them. I structured the situation because people who have trouble with reality need and want structure. I gave them structure, but I set the limits a little more advanced than the ward routine permitted or required. First, we voted on whether the time was agreeable. The librarian and I had previously decided that there would be three times that she and I could attend. We did *not* say to these people, "You can meet any time you want," but we did explain to the group why the co-leaders had previously selected the three possible choices of time. The group's decision, which included the votes of the co-leaders, was to retain the meeting at 6:30 on Thursday evening for one hour. The co-leaders planned to confer for a half hour after each meeting.

During the first meeting, the group discussed what we might want to do and talk about in the future. One woman said she was reading a book and would like to report on it in several weeks. Thus, we had the nucleus of a program set up for three weeks hence. We structured and enhanced her voluntary participation by saying, "Three weeks from now, Susie Jones will give a book review." We told her that she would have as much time as she needed or desired. If she didn't want to use the whole meeting, we would help her by talking about the book on which she reported. Thus, the initial meeting of the group bibliotherapy project was spent in a reassuring, structuring, getting-acquainted fashion. To these qualities, the co-therapists added their appreciation and recognition of the members' special efforts and accomplishment. At the end of the meeting, I suggested that we have some refreshment. One of the two women who had not been off the ward in three years asked if she might help. This same lady later said, "Maybe next week I can provide some of the refreshments."

No patient volunteered to speak for the second meeting and so I said I would. At that time, I was studying Interlingua, so I decided to give a discussion on that topic. I brought the blackboard in a little bit, stood up and talked for 30 minutes about Interlingua and a common language for all mankind. I attempted to get the patients involved. The librarian generally sat across the room from where I sat. Thus, when she spoke, the patients' eyes were on her, and when I spoke, the patients looked over and across the circle to me. In this way, patients were forced to see other patients even if out of the corner of the eyes. This awareness is one of the important benefits of circular seating. Also, no one talks to the back of somebody's head as would occur if we had sat in rows of chairs.

After several months, other patients requested that they be included in the group. Eventually, we had a group of 15 women patients. We invited other doctors to send some of their patients. The enthusiasm spread, and eventually men asked if they, too, could participate. The administrative officials deliberated a long time as to the advisability of allowing closed ward patients and open ward patients in the same project. The officials finally allowed mixing of patients from the open and closed wards and eventually men and women in the same bibliotherapy group. (A revolutionary step for those days.)

We did not force patients to talk, participate, or give a speech. However, we encouraged and guided them into involvement. One of the few rules we made was that the patients deal with the situation as realistically as possible within this group setting. Gradually, the group began to develop and exert certain social standards within itself. For example, many men wore ties and the women were dressed up; the men moved the furniture and the women served the refreshments.

The co-leaders always had something prepared so we could give a presentation without notice. We tried to give patients sufficient advance notice of the time and date for their talk. We would always do this at the end of the preceding meeting but would try to refer to the agenda for the following two or three weeks whenever possible. For the speaker, we arranged a podium near the speaker's desk. If a patient was scheduled to talk about a certain book, the librarian would prepare a display of other books or works by that author or some other related material. This exhibit was assembled in advance so when the patients walked into the meeting, they would be able to see and examine the material even before the speaker started his presentation. This exhibit was kept on display for the following week, with a special sign relating to the patients' bibliotherapy group. Generally at first, one of the co-leaders introduced the speaker; later patient-members took turns chairing the meetings.

For one meeting, when no patient was scheduled to talk, the librarian and I selected a short play with two characters. She read one role and I read the other. The next week, we selected a three-part play. A patient, who volunteered for the task, joined the librarian and me in reading the roles. The following week, the group got interested in the procedure and so we read a four-part comedy. We gave the two main roles to patients. One was the patient who had read the previous week and a second patient volunteered.

Later, we had a five-part play at which time I dropped out of the reading. It was arranged to give each participant a copy of the play a week ahead of time. We tried to select plays for which we had four or five copies. Otherwise, we mimeographed copies or the patients typed carbons. (This was in the days before Xerox.) As much as possible, we allowed and encouraged the patients to do this preparatory work. After awhile, we had eight-part readings in which the librarian and I did not participate.

Some patients felt a reluctance to take active part in the group reading or in a book review or discussion. We wondered if they would feel better (safer?) if they could privately tape record their "speech" and have it presented to the group at the next regular meeting. Thus, we arranged for some of the patients to go to the recording studio and tape record a book report. Most wrote it in long hand and read it into the recorder. At the next meeting, the patient would be introduced in the regular manner. He would sit near the speaker's podium, the display would be arranged in the usual manner, and we would play the tape recording instead of having the patient speak "live." After the patient gave this talk by tape, we would carry on as if he had given it live. One person made four tape recordings before she was able to give a live report. That was a triumphant occasion for her and the start of "her road back to emotional health." We tried to give each person the opportunity to come back gradually to the world of reality; to see and test for himself whether the world was safe.

Another approach was inviting each member to list the three pieces of literature "most meaningful" to him. The Bible was a favorite selection. Shakespeare was often a second choice. The three choices of each patient gave us additional insight into his personality and interests. I later suggested that each person speak for one and one-half minutes and give reasons why he chose these three selections. There were about 18 members present that evening, even though they had been given advance warning of at least one week as to the requirements and expectations of the one and one-half minute speech. At that meeting, each person was *obligated* to speak. We did not allow him the privilege to refuse to speak. Four patients at this meeting had been members about four months, but none of them had ever spoken. None had entered a cross discussion or had ever made a comment. We did not allow these people at that point to have a choice because the rule of the group at that meeting was that everyone made a comment. We had, of course, told them one week earlier of the change in the "therapeutic contract." Since they were in attendance, we had the right to assume they were willing to abide by the new format. They had to speak, if only to say, "I don't really know." Even though two or three were reluctant, they nonetheless spoke. Moreover, they spoke in a group, exchanged ideas, and were receptive to other people's remarks.

Another thing we did with increasing skill was to help the patients gain prestige. We helped them to become important. We invited some well-known people to be our guest speakers. Dr. Karl Menninger, who has always been enthusiastic about bibliotherapy, and who had watched our group with supportive interest, read some poetry to us. We had a paraplegic author discuss his book with us. Suitable publicity was arranged in the hospital newspaper for these "invitational meetings." Each member was permitted to invite two guests, and the evening was a special one for all concerned. We also suggested to certain patients that they meet the guest speaker at the front entrance hall, escort him to the library, and introduce him as the speaker of the evening.

Quite often, we used forms of literature other than books. Movies were occasionally employed such as a movie that had to do with literature or one that might blend in with the topic that one of the members discussed. One of the patients spoke about "mobiles," and we used a film on mobiles, a beautiful symphony in color, movement, and music.

We used tape recording a great deal. A patient had given an excellent review of a biography of Albert Schweitzer. Some months earlier, I had heard a radio program concerning Dr. Schweitzer. I borrowed a transcription of this program and we played the tape for a whole meeting. Other members of the group wanted to talk more about Dr. Schweitzer; for seven consecutive meetings, different members spoke about that wonderfully inspirational person. We had used a book report originally as an approach to a tape recording which, in turn, was an entree into verbalizing and then into interpersonal communication.

Within a two-year span, group membership fluctuated between five and 20, averaged out from 12 to 15, with overall attendance around 95%. We found we were most comfortable with around 12 people. For those who were too withdrawn and frightened to function in this original group, we formed a secondary literary discussion group composed of the more chronic, withdrawn, isolated, and insulated patients. This group met during the day in case they required attendants. We limited this group to seven or eight and structured it much more than the original group. In this structured group of more regressed patients, extensive use was made of the *Reader's Digest* with each person having his own copy. One patient would read a paragraph, another would read the next, and so on around the circle. It was important to allow each individual to have something he could call his own, even if it was only the privilege of reading a paragraph, *his* paragraph from *his Reader's Digest*. We also benefitted from passing a book around, thus initiating physical and psychological contact. If one patient handed another a book and the second was "out of this world" (daydreaming-fantasizing-hallucinating), then the first patient got the attention of the other and had to say "here" and show him the proper place.

Lessons Learned

We soon learned the advisability of not allowing our patients to choose literature indiscriminately, and of the need of our guiding them into selecting material not disturbing to other patients. One example of indiscriminate selection was by a man who suffered from a manic psychosis. He chose to describe the erotic art of Pompeii, and his description was too harsh and startling for many patients. The co-leaders soon found that it was worthwhile to always have collateral knowledge of the subject about which the patient was going to speak. This knowing beforehand often enabled the therapists to shift into a more socially acceptable facet of the discussion.

Although not absolutely essential, a psychiatrist can be extremely useful on the bibliotherapeutic team. My own psychiatric training, for example, enables me to understand the dynamics of the individual illness of the patient and the dynamics of the group interchange. Certainly, the psychiatrist can help the librarian better understand the pathological state of interaction as well as the normal state of group and individual behavior. However, psychiatrists are not the only people who try to understand human behavior. Many professionals of allied disciplines are interested and capable in this area. In any event, it is unfair and unreasonable to expect the librarian to know about the dynamics of mental illness and apply that knowledge with the same skill as a trained psychiatrist, psychologist, social worker, or sociologist. It is absolutely essential that there be some member of the bibliotherapeutic team who is qualified and willing to share his knowledge of emotional and mental illness and personality struggles with the other members.

Let us be realistic about bibliotherapy. Not everybody believes in it. Some professionals seem to resent the term. Although I am convinced that literature is a unique and profitable modality in the treatment of mentally ill people, I don't think it will entirely replace psycho-pharmacological utilization (medication), or the appearance of a nurse or volunteer on a ward, or electroconvulsive shock treatment, or psychotherapy, or three meals a day. I don't think bibliotherapy can necessarily take the place of protective screening which some patients seem to require to feel safe. Bibliotherapy is just one more technique that we can use if we are so inclined. We must educate doctors, just as much as we educate others, in the efficacy of using literature therapeutically.

Closing Reflections

I have described some historical as well as practical considerations in the use of literature as a therapeutic tool in a group process in a mental hospital. It has not been my intention to "sell anything." I have tried to acquaint the reader with an additional method or tool with which to treat patients. Space limitations did not permit me to discuss many other important areas in the bibliotherapeutic armamentarium. For example, I have not dealt at all with individual biblio-therapy—that is, with the actual prescription of a certain book for a certain patient to get across one idea.

In closing, I sincerely hope that there will be many readers of this chapter who will be stimulated to do bibliotherapy research. We must develop additional effective bibliotherapy training programs. There must be continuing inquiry by the individual general therapist as to the nature of what bibliotheraphy is, how it can be used, replicated, and evaluated, and how significant numbers of trained people can utilize it effectively.

References

Geisel, Theodor Seuss. *Yertle the turtle and other stories*. New York: Random House, 1958.

CHAPTER 12

Approaching Poetry Therapy
from a Scientific Orientation*

Franklin M. Berry

Introduction

What has come to be known as poetry therapy is by no means a well-defined technique. There are in fact several different contemporary versions of poetry therapy. Some of these appear to have little in common except for the fact that poetry is being used in some way to help people work out their problems. The bipartite division of the field into models of poetry therapy which emphasize the reading of pre-existing poems versus models which emphasize the writing of new poems is a case in point (see Harrower, 1974). The presently diverging views of poetry therapy were captured nicely in a recent editorial: " . . . the observer [is] confronted with an olio of approaches, endeavors, skills and training, manifested in diverse settings, ranging from little or no professional involvement and supervision to the more sophisticated and carefully monitored variety" (Lerner, 1976, p. i).

Poetry therapy is also in a state of uncertainty with particular reference to other currently practiced therapies. One source of this uncertainty concerns poetry therapy's relation to nonliterary therapies; another concerns its relation to other currently practiced literature-based therapies, using books, short stories, and one-act plays. With respect to the views involving nonliterary therapies, one finds poetry therapy conceptualized by some (e.g., Leedy, 1969, Chapter 5) as an "adjunctive therapy" analogous to art, dance, or music therapy, and by others (e.g., Shiryon, 1976) as a full or complete method of psychotherapy in its own right. With respect to the other literature-based therapies, one finds writers holding widely divergent views of how poetry

*This chapter is dedicated to the memory of my friend and colleague, Dr. Terry R. Anders, 1940-1974, whose untimely death propelled me into the domain of poetry therapy.

therapy is related to bibliotherapy or literatherapy. Some writers treat poetry as identical to bibliotherapy (e.g., Moody & Limper, 1971) or to bibliotherapy *and* literatherapy (e.g., Monroe & Rubin, 1975). Other writers see poetry therapy as a part of bibliotherapy (e.g., Lerner, 1973) or a part of literatherapy (e.g., Shiryon, 1972, 1976). A third group of writers considers poetry therapy a separate therapeutic profession requiring independent certification (e.g., Leedy, 1969).

Therapeutically speaking, one is tempted to do his own thing, given the problems of distinguishing poetry therapy from bibliotherapy, poetry therapy from literatherapy, and bibliotherapy from literatherapy. Following this easier course appears to have been the norm for the clinical practitioner faced with immediate demands for therapy. The poetry therapist has done poetry therapy, and for the most part ignored bibliotherapy, and the bibliotherapist has done likewise. It seems obvious that in the future, poetry therapists and bibliotherapists will have to communicate better if serious progress is to be made toward the goal of creating a truly comprehensive field of literature-based therapies.

The Empirical Phase of Our Research: Initial Pilot Investigations*

At the outset, it ought to be emphasized that these initial investigations were not concerned with evaluation of the clinical practice of poetry therapy either with respect to the validation of poetry therapy as therapy *qua* therapy or with respect to the relative efficiency of poetry therapy compared to other types of therapy (although this sort of study is sorely needed). Nor were our initial researches concerned with a process-level understanding of what goes on in the different versions of poetry therapy. Rather, the intent of the present series of studies was to try to get a handle on the possible roles that people's reading and/or writing behaviors may play in their attempts to cope with life (Pilot Study 1). Another purpose of these studies was determining whether it is possible to objectify the means by which a therapist selects a poem to present to a patient. The objectifying is accomplished here by sets of empirical norms of feelings evoked by the reading of pre-existing written poetry (Pilot Study 2).

---

*The author wishes to acknowledge the collaboration of his students, Beth Ellis, Jan Heyn, and Chuck Lanham, in the research activities described in this chapter; Beth Ellis for her contribution to the bibliography-building efforts (e.g., Ellis & Berry, 1976), Jan Heyn for her contribution to the general survey of reading and writing behaviors (Heyn & Berry, 1976), and Chuck Lanham for his contribution to the poetry-processing work focusing on feelings (Lanham & Berry, 1976). Their contribution to this research is deeply valued and appreciated by the "principal investigator."

Pilot Study 1:
A Survey Focusing on Reading and Writing Behaviors
of College Students
Both in General and in Times of Crisis

As we became familiar with some of the literature on poetry therapy and bibliotherapy, we were impressed by the dearth of empirical evidence supporting the efficacy of either technique. In the same vein, there appears to have been little in the way of empirical work on the problem of understanding the role played by poetry or other forms of literature in facilitating the therapeutic encounter.

The present study was, therefore, designed to gain empirical information relevant to the practice of poetry therapy or bibliotherapy. The idea was to get some preliminary information about the reading and writing behaviors of adults, in general and in response to crisis, and by so doing contribute to the development of a much needed empirical foundation for the practice of poetry therapy or bibliotherapy. It seems clear to the present writer that major advances in the poetry therapy-bibliotherapy field will require that anecdotal approaches be supplemented by empirical ones.

We began our work by asking college students what they read or wrote, how much they read or wrote, and whether or not they had ever read or written something to help themselves through a crisis. In a way, the reading-in-crisis, writing-in-crisis portion of our survey was directed at determining whether poetry therapy or bibliotherapy occurs spontaneously among adult readers. That is, this portion of our survey was designed to tell us whether some adults could be expected to have learned to use reading and/or writing behaviors as coping mechanisms in crisis situations. Although the idea did not occur to us at the beginning of this study, it later seemed obvious that knowing something about a person's reading and/or writing history ought to be a good predictor of how amenable this person would be to poetry therapy or bibliotherapy.

Method

Subjects. The subjects were 27 male and female introductory psychology students at Columbus College. Most students were college sophomores with a mean age of 20.1 years and standard deviation of 2.0 years. These students participated in the study in order to complete a laboratory assignment.

Materials. Two questionnaires were constructed to generate three different kinds of information: (1) demographic information, such as age, sex, year in school, and grade point average; (2) information on the students' reading and writing behaviors in general; and (3) information on the students' reading and writing behaviors in a crisis situation (that is, following either the death of a significant other person or the death of a pet). The questionnaires contained items directed toward reading, writing, and publishing different types of literature (Have you ever written a poem? How many? How many published?), and items directed toward reading/writing behaviors in crisis (What was the nature of the death faced? Whose death was involved? How was literature used to cope with the crisis?).

Results

Table 12-1 presents frequency distributions of student status, sex, class standing, and race. As can be seen, the majority of students were college sophomores, there are slightly more females than males, most students placed in the middle of their class, and all but three students were white. In addition, the students' mean grade point average (4.0 system) was 2.8 (SD=.6) and their mean introductory psychology course grade was also 2.8 (SD=1.1).

Tables 12-2 and 12-3 show the different frequency distributions of general reading behaviors and of general writing behaviors, respectively. A close inspection of Table 12-2 will reveal that on the average, 70% of the students read short stories, poems, and novels, while 94.5% read newspapers and magazines. A comparison of these averages indicates that there are a number of students who read only newspapers and magazines. The final two categories, "Bible" and "Plays," were suggested by the students. A similar inspection of Table 12-3 will show that at least one form of writing behavior, that of writing poems or essays, was demonstrated by (17/27) 63% of the students. It is also interesting to note the quantity of material produced, especially in the category of "Poems" where

Table 12-1 Frequency Distributions of Student Status, Sex, Class Standing, and Race

Category	Frequency
Student Status	
Freshmen	7
Sophomores	15
Juniors	5
Seniors	0
Sex	
Male	11
Female	16
Class Standing	
Upper	8
Middle	17
Lower	2
Race	
Black	3
White	24

Table 12-2   Frequency Distributions of General Reading Behaviors (materials read for pleasure in the last calendar year)

Type Read	People (No.)	People (%)	No. Read
Short story	21 (20)*	78 (74)*	316 (266)*
Poems	18 (17)*	67 (63)*	1151 (751)*
Novels	18 (17)*	67 (83)*	118 (108)*
Drama	0	0	0
Magazine articles	25	93	1476
Newspapers	26	96	8840
"Bible"	3	11	N/A
"Plays"	1	04	5

Note: Quotes indicate those categories suggested by the students themselves.
(Totals for the No. People column exceed 27 because the categories are not mutually exclusive.)
*Totals obtained when one highly prolific writer is ignored.

Table 12-3   Frequency Distributions of General Writing Behaviors (considering each respondent's entire life and only *nonschool-related* productions)

Type Written	People (No.)	People (%)	No. Produced
Poem	17 (16)*	63 (59)*	676 (145)*
Short story	9 (8)*	33 (30)*	50 (20)*
Novel	1 (0)*	04 (0)*	1 (1)*
Novella	0	0	0
Song	1	04	2
Nursery rhyme	0	0	0
"Essay"	1	04	3
"Play"	1	04	1
"Letters to no one"	1	04	(unspecified)
None (don't write)	9	33	N/A

Note: Quotes indicate those categories suggested by the students themselves.
(Totals for the No. People column exceed 27 because the categories are not mutually exclusive.)
*Totals obtained when one highly prolific writer is ignored.

17 students produced a total of 676 poems. It must be pointed out, however, that one student contributed a disproportionate number of poems—531. When we ignored this prolific writer, we found that 16 people produced 145 poems, which is an average of 9.1 poems per person. Again, quotes indicate those types of literary productions that were suggested by the students themselves. The last category includes 33% of the students who do not write.

Table 12-4   Frequency Distribution of Why the "Writers" (N=18) Said They Wrote

Category	People (No.)	People (%)
Fun	11	61
See if I could	6	33
See if I could get published	2	11
Compelled	6	33
Prestige	0	0
"Expression"	4	22
"Relieve feelings"	1	06
"Pressure"	1	06

Note: Quotes indicate those categories suggested by the students themselves. (Totals exceed 18 because categories are not mutually exclusive.)

Table 12-4 presents a frequency distribution of replies to a section of the survey concerned with why those people who said they were writers chose to write. Sixty-one percent of the 18 writers stated they wrote for fun; 33% said they wrote to see if they could; and another 33% said they wrote because they felt compelled to. None of the students said they wrote for the prestige of being a writer.

The results of that portion of the survey dealing with the use of literature and/or writing of literature in time of crisis are presented in Table 12-5. A close inspection of this table will reveal that a total of 10 of the 27 students used literature in some fashion as a coping resource. Four of the students, who read or wrote or read *and* wrote, clearly made a primary literary response to a death. Two others made what might be called a secondary literary response by recalling something they had read earlier to facilitate working through the "current crisis." The remaining four made both a primary and a secondary response. In addition, six of these 10 students who made "literary responses" indicated that they thought of this strategy themselves, and so might be said to have practiced bibliotherapy spontaneously. The other four practiced bibliotherapy on advice from someone else.

Table 12-6 presents the results of an extensive correlational analysis we undertook as an attempt to gain some sort of closure concerning the students' reported reading and writing behaviors. For example, Total Literature Read was correlated with Grade Point Average, Course Grade and Total ("Literature") Written and where applicable separate correlations were calculated for "Writers Only" (i.e., those students who created literary productions as part of their general lifestyle). For ease of interpretation, the corresponding means and SDs of the various measures analyzed are also provided. Inspection of Table 12-6 will reveal that only four correlations proved significant. Of these, only three are related to reading/writing behaviors and all of them involve Total Literature Read correlated with other measures. More specifically, Total Literature Read correlated positively with grade point average, $r = .43$, with df = 25, $p < .05$; and with total written, $r = .88$, with df = 25, $p < .01$, considering all subjects; and with total written, $r = .89$, with df = 16, $p < .01$, considering Writers Only.

The correlations between Total Written and Total Literature Read are of particular interest in the context of poetry therapy or bibliotherapy. When it is recalled (from Table 12-4) that only 18 of the students actually created literary productions and thereby had numbers larger than zero entered into these correlations (first, considering all subjects and second, considering Writers Only), it becomes clear that the extremely high obtained correlations of .88 versus .89, respectively, are principally the result of the fact that our writers also tend to be readers. A comparison of the means of Total Literature Read for all subjects and for Writers Only, 58.7 (SD=95.1) versus 80.9 (SD=110.4), also supports this view. Moreover, when only the nine non-writers are considered, the mean of

Table 12-5 Frequency Distribution of "Literary Responses" in Time of Crisis (where the crisis faced was the death of a significant other person or pet)

Crisis Activity	No. People
Read	2
Wrote	1
Read and wrote	1
Re-experienced something previously read	2
Read or wrote *and* re-experienced something previously read	4
No literary activity	17

Table 12-6 Table of Pearson Product-Moment Correlation Coefficients Between Various Measures

Category	$\overline{X}$	SD	r	p
Grade Point Average	2.7	.6		
Course grade	2.8	1.0	.56	<.01
Total literature read	58.7	95.1	.43	<.05
Total magazines and newspapers read	380.4	176.2	-.11	NS
Total written	27.2	101.3	.30	NS
Total written (writers only)	40.7	122.9	.28	NS
Course Grade	2.8	1.0		
Total literature read	58.7	95.1	.24	NS
Total magazines and newspapers read	380.4	176.2	-.21	NS
Total written	27.2	101.3	.24	NS
Total written (writers only)	40.7	122.9	.28	NS
Total Written	27.2	101.3		
Total literature read	58.7	95.1	.88	<.01
Total magazines and newspapers read	380.4	176.2	-.02	NS
Total crisis situations	1.9	1.2	.08	NS
Total Written (Writers Only)				
Total literature read (writers only)	80.9	110.4	.89	<.01
Total crisis situations (writers only)	2.1	1.3	.04	NS

(N = 27 in all categories except Writers Only, in which N = 18)

Total Literature Read drops to 12.3 (SD=14.2). The large discrepancy in amount of literature read for writers versus non-writers still remains even when the one extremely prolific writer is not considered; the other 17 writers' mean of Total Literature Read was 58.7 (SD=56.6), a value which is still about four times as large as that for non-writers. This difference is obviously significant despite the considerable skewing in both distributions.

For our last analysis, we decided to follow-up on the entirely reasonable notion that our writers ought to be more likely than our non-writers to actually turn to literature in time of crisis. A 2 x 2 contingency table was constructed by contrasting writers and non-writers on their use or non-use of bibliotherapy. Table 12-7 summarizes this analysis. The category, Bibliotherapy Used, represents a combination of the primary, secondary, and combined literary responses to crisis categories listed in Table 12-5. Likewise, the category, Bibliotherapy Not Used, represents the students in the "No Literary Activity" category of Table 12-5.

An inspection of Table 12-7 will show that whereas (9/18) 50% of the writers used bibliotherapy, only (1/9) 13% of the non-writers did so. Quite obviously there was a significant relationship between these categorical dimensions, x^2 (with 1 df) = 3.9, $p < .05$.

Discussion

The results of the present study suggest that knowledge of a person's general frequency of reading and/or writing of literature may prove useful in the conduct of poetry therapy or bibliotherapy. We saw that total literature read correlated very highly with total literature written—that is, high frequency readers produce more written productions (or vice versa) and, also, that if one is a writer he is likely to turn to literature in the face of crisis with writers being more likely than non-writers to turn to literature (reading/writing/recalling

Table 12-7   A 2 X 2 Contingency Table Contrasting Writers and Non-Writers and Their Use or Non-Use of Bibliotherapy in Response to Crisis

	Bibliotherapy Used	Bibliotherapy Not Used	
Writers	Expected value = 6.7 Obtained = 9	Expected value = 11.3 Obtained = 9	18
Non-Writers	Expected value = 3.3 Obtained = 1	Expected value = 5.7 Obtained = 8	9
	10	17	

something previously read or some combination of these) as an aid in coping with the death of a significant other person or pet. It is to be expected that writer/non-writer status would be predictive of the likelihood of a literary response to other types of crises as well, although we have no data on this matter.

Our results also seem to have some bearing on the practice of poetry therapy or bibliotherapy as therapy *qua* therapy. It would be expected that persons with a high operant literature-reading level or a high operant literature-writing level would quickly take to a therapy based on such behaviors. Indeed, one might expect that people who already write would be highly amenable to forms of therapy which place emphasis on creative writing. Likewise, people who have a history of reading literature might be expected to be particularly susceptible to forms of therapy which place emphasis on reading pre-existing written literature.

A related implication concerns both group poetry therapy and group bibliotherapy. Given the results of the present study it would seem strategic that prior to the onset of therapy, groups be so structured that they will contain some members who read literature and/or do creative writing. If such procedure is followed, non-readers or non-writers will be better prepared for the kind of behavior appropriate to the group experience.

Although the present study is only a beginning, it does give us some insight into adult reading and writing behaviors and their possible import for poetry therapy and bibliotherapy. There is also the question of how effectively such forms of therapy can be used with those people who do not read or write as part of their general lifestyle. The importance of this question is further underscored by the fact that people in general are probably less likely to read and/or write than the community college students surveyed here.

Pilot Study 2:
An Exploratory Investigation of Poetry Interpretation by College Students

In Pilot Study 2 we were concerned with the problem of generating an empirical base with which to approach the important problem of matching-up people and poems. That this problem is a general one is attested to by the fact that poem-prescription can play a prominent role in most of the different versions of poetry therapy. This important problem has been dealt with by a number of writers (e.g., Blanton, 1960; Leedy, 1969; Schloss, 1976). However, only one of these has attempted to generate an empirically derived classification of poems for use as a guide to poetry therapists in their attempts to match-up people and poems (see Schloss, 1976, Chapter 15).

Method

Subjects. Twenty-seven college students enrolled in an Introductory Psychology class served as subjects in order to complete a laboratory assignment.

Materials. Five poems were selected at random from an anthology of 287 poems prepared by Mrs. Vi Jaster, Cleveland Psychiatric Institute for use in her poetry therapy sessions: "Stopping by Woods on a Snowy Evening" (Robert Frost), "The Fruit of the Spirit is Love and Peace" (Helen Steiner Rice), "When I was One and Twenty" (A. E. Houseman), "The Garden Year" (Sara Coleridge), and "Seeing Eye to Eye is Believing" (Ogden Nash). A questionnaire (rating sheet) was constructed which addressed itself principally to how interpretation was achieved (e.g., was it based on the title, one line, one stanza or the whole poem, and so on) and what feelings resulted from each interpretation (e.g., tenderness, pity, disgust, sad, happy, anger, that nature is beautiful, and so on). The last questionnaire item called for the subject to indicate how well he liked the poem on a 5-point rating scale which ranged from "Didn't Like It At All" to "Liked It a Lot."

Procedure. Each subject was provided a folder containing the five pre-selected poems and the rating sheets. The order of appearance of the poems in each folder was random with a questionnaire following each poem. The experimenter asked each person to remove the first poem and questionnaire, then to read the poem and rate it. After all subjects had completed the first poem, the experimenter directed the subjects to turn them over and to follow the same procedure with the remaining poems.

Results

Table 12-8 illustrates the role that form was avowed to play in attaining an interpretation of each poem and on evoking feelings. As can be seen, the entire poem is said to be most important in generating an interpretation and in accounting for the feelings the poem evokes in the reader. Next in line of importance is the title and some single stanza of the poem, but these categories are not checked with anywhere near the frequency of the whole poem.

As our next step, we looked at how each poem was rated on a 5-point scale of absolute preference. Figure 12-1 depicts how the poems were ordered on this scale. We expanded that portion of the scale ranging from a rating of 2 to a rating of 3 for clarity. Frost's poem, "Stopping by Woods on a Snowy Evening" achieved the highest absolute preference rating, followed by Rice's poem, "The Fruit of the Spirit is Love and Peace," Houseman's, "When I was One and Twenty," Coleridge's, "The Garden Year," and finally, Nash's, "Seeing Eye to Eye is Believing." A one-way analysis of variance for repeated measures was performed on the preference ratings assigned to these five poems. The F, df=4/104, was 4.6, which is significant at $p < .01$. A simple main effect breakdown revealed that the following pairs of poems were significantly

Table 12-8 How Subjects Say Poetic Form Affects Poem Interpretation and Influences Feeling Evocation

	Poem Interpretation*								
	Visual Form	One Word	One Phrase	One Stanza	One Line	Title	Whole Poem	Other	Don't Know
Rice	6	— —	— —	2	1	5	20	3	1
Nash	3	2	2	3	2	5	16	3	— —
Coleridge	2	— —	— —	— —	— —	4	19	1	— —
Houseman	1	1	3	7	3	4	19	2	— —
Frost	6	2	3	5	2	4	18	2	— —
Totals	18	5	8	17	8	22	92	11	1 = 182
Percent of Grand Total	10	3	4	9	4	12	51	6	1

	Feeling Evocation*								
	Visual Form	One Word	One Phrase	One Stanza	One Line	Title	Whole Poem	Other	Don't Know
Rice	3	— —	— —	4	1	6	20	1	1
Nash	2	— —	2	2	— —	5	14	1	1
Coleridge	5	— —	— —	— —	— —	2	20	2	— —
Houseman	2	— —	5	4	3	4	14	— —	— —
Frost	4	— —	1	5	2	5	22	1	1
Totals	16	0	8	15	6	22	90	5	3 = 165
Percent of Grand Total	10	0	5	9	4	13	54	3	2

*Subjects could give more than one answer per poem.

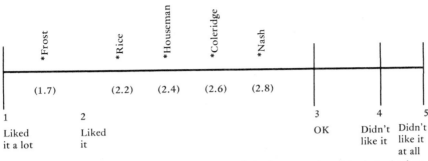

Fig. 12-1. The ordering of the five poems studied along a scale of (mean) absolute preference. (Note that the portion of the scale from 2-3 has been expanded out of proportion for clarity *and* that the scale runs from 1, indicating high preference, to 5, indicating low preference.)

different in average absolute preference (all comparisons $p < .05$): Frost versus Houseman, Frost versus Coleridge, Frost versus Nash, and Rice versus Nash. In addition, the comparison of Frost versus Rice approached significance, t (104 df) = 1.9, $p < .10$. Looking again at Fig. 12-1, the results of this analysis suggest that only the points 1.7, 2.2 (or 2.4), and 2.8 are truly different points of preference.

As our next step, we examined the total number of feelings evoked by each poem and then we attempted to determine whether the patterns of feeling evocation were related to the ordering of the poems on the scale of absolute preference. Table 12-9 presents the means and SDs of the total number of feelings elicited by each poem. Inspection of Table 12-9 will reveal that the more preferred poems tended to evoke more feelings. Recalling that only four preference comparisons yielded significant differences, we performed four t tests on the corresponding means of feelings evoked. These comparisons (N=27 per comparison) and the resulting t values were: Frost versus Houseman, $t=2.2$; Frost versus Coleridge, $t=.9$; Frost versus Nash, $t=2.5$; and Rice versus Nash, $t=2.3$. All of these differences were significant at $p < .05$ except for the Frost versus Coleridge comparison.

Table 12-9 Means and SDs of Total Number of Feelings Evoked by Each Poem

Poet/Poem	Mean	SD
Frost's ("Stopping By Woods . . . ")	3.3	1.9
Rice's ("Fruit of the Spirit . . . ")	3.3	2.4
Houseman's (". . . One and Twenty")	2.2	1.7
Coleridge's ("The Garden Year")	2.7	2.3
Nash's ("Seeing Eye to Eye . . . ")	1.9	2.2

Given this analysis, it seems reasonable to conclude that a poem's preference rating is strongly influenced by the number of feelings which that poem evokes in the reader. However, as a further check on this hypothesis, we calculated Pearson product-moment correlation coefficients between preference ratings and the number of feelings evoked for each of the five poems. Table 12-10 shows the obtained correlations. Again we find evidence for a poem's preference rating being at least partially determined by its ability to evoke feelings.

Table 12-10   Correlations Between Preference Ratings and Number of Feelings Evoked for Each Poem

Poet/Poem	r	p
Frost ("Stopping")	- .38	< .10
Rice ("Spirit")	- .58	< .01
Houseman ("One and Twenty")	- .18	N.S.
Coleridge ("Garden")	- .43	< .05
Nash ("Eye")	- .41	< .05

Note: Correlations are negative because a low number on the preference scale meant a high preference. (N = 27 for each comparison.)

Discussion

The results of the present study seem to indicate that a poem's subjective value (that is, how much it is liked by an adult reader) is directly related to the frequency with which it evokes feelings in that reader. Most of the preference rating comparisons between those poems which actually differed in preferential value support this interpretation. Likewise, most of the correlations involving preference value and number of evoked feelings also support this view. Although it is not possible to gauge the strength of this relationship very accurately, given the limitations of the present study, our small sample, our crude feeling categories, and our small collection of poems, we can provide at least a rough estimation by averaging the coefficients of determination for the five obtained correlations. The resulting estimate is that about 17% of the variance in poem preference ratings can be accounted for by the single covariate of frequency of feelings elicited. It seems reasonable to expect that a "cleaner" study might reveal a stronger relationship between feelings evoked by a poem and its perceived subjective value.

Finally, we want to make explicit the possible relevance of Pilot Study 2 findings to the practice of poetry therapy. The present results suggest that given some further refinements in our approach to assessing a poem's capacity to evoke feelings, we may be able in the future to describe accurately the feeling-evocation properties of a poem.

Table 12-11   High Incidence Feelings for the Five Poems Rated
(a prototype poem classification based on feelings evoked)

FROST		RICE		HOUSEMAN		COLERIDGE		NASH	
Feeling	%R	Feeling	%R	Feeling	%R	Feeling	%R	Feeling	%R
Nature is beautiful	70	Hopeful	52	Life is complicated	30	Nature is beautiful	63	Life is complicated	33
Lonely	44	Life has meaning	44			Feel good	37		
Relaxed	41	Life is complicated	37			Glad to be alive	37		

Note: There were 27 respondents (Rs) who rated each poem; also, the criterion for inclusion in this table was that more than 25% of the respondents chose the feeling as appropriate to the poem.

Table 12-11 presents a prototype of the kind of empirical classification of poems that would be most useful to a poetry therapist who is attempting to select an "appropriate" poem to present to a given individual. Armed with Table 12-11, our future poetry therapist could prescribe either Frost's poem or Coleridge's poem for a person the therapist believes needs to experience the wonder of nature or loneliness and Rice's poem for a person the therapist feels needs to experience hope or that life has meaning.

Concluding Remarks

With regard to future research efforts in the poetry therapy-bibliotherapy field, the results of Pilot Study 2 are particularly provocative. They suggest that it may indeed be possible to establish a normative classification of poems to be used in objectifying the process of poem-prescription based on feelings evoked by the poems. This line of research needs to be followed up by large-scale investigations based on many poems, much larger samples (say, N=100 raters per poem) and improved procedures for assessing a poem's capacity to evoke feelings. Factor-analytic methods may prove highly useful in subsequent attempts to improve assessment of evoked feelings. For example, some sort of cluster analysis might be used to reduce a large number of apparently different feelings to a much smaller number of truly different feelings.

While it is impossible to predict just what the future has in store for the poetry therapy-bibliotherapy area, it seems entirely reasonable to expect that application of the methods of science to this field will greatly facilitate its development. This is not to say that intuitive and/or artistic approaches to poetry therapy or bibliotherapy will be supplanted by scientific approaches or devalued as a result of them, but rather that intuitive and/or artistic approaches are to be complemented by scientific approaches. The present author is just enough of a poet to realize how important nonrational processes are in the practice of poetry therapy.

References

Blanton, Smiley. *The healing power of poetry*. New York: Crowell, 1960.

Ellis, L. B., & Berry, F. M. "A partial listing of sources related to bibliotherapy and poetry therapy: A second run at a comprehensive listing." Mimeo, 64 pages, 1976.

Harrower, Molly. "The therapy of poetry." *Current Psychiatric Therapies*, 1974, *14*, 97-105.

Heyn, J. E., & Berry, F. M. "Reading and writing behaviors of college students: A pilot study." Paper presented at the Annual Meeting of the Georgia Psychological Association, Columbus, 1976.

Lanham, C., & Berry, F. M. "Poetry interpretation by college students: A pilot study." Paper presented at the Annual Meeting of the Georgia Psychological Association, Columbus, 1976.

Leedy, J. J. (Ed.) *Poetry therapy*. Philadelphia: Lippincott, 1969a.

Leedy, J. J. "Principles of poetry therapy." In J. J. Leedy (Ed.), *Poetry therapy*, Philadelphia: Lippincott, 1969b. Pp. 67-74.

Lerner, A. "Editorial: A look at poetry therapy." *Art Psychotherapy*, 1976, *3*, i-ii.

Lerner, A. "Poetry therapy." *American Journal of Nursing*, 1973, *73*, 1336-1338.

Monroe, M. E., & Rubin, R. J. "Bibliotherapy: Trends in the United States." *Health and Rehabilitation*, 1975, *1*, 15-17.

Moody, M., & Limper, H. K. *Bibliotherapy methods and materials*. Chicago: American Library Association, 1971.

Schloss, G. A. *Psychopoetry*. New York: Grosset & Dunlap, 1976.

Shiryon, M. "25 years of bibliotherapy." Paper presented at the 25th Annual Convention of the California State Psychological Association, Los Angeles, 1972.

Shiryon, M. "Biblical roots of literatherapy." Paper presented at the 56th Annual Convention of the Western Psychological Association, Los Angeles, 1976.

INDEX

The Library
University of California
JUN 8 2001   *Riverside*

THIS BOOK IS DUE ON THE LAST DATE STAMPED BELOW
Books not returned on time are subject to fines according
to the Library Lending Code.
Books cannot be renewed by phone.
Books may be recalled at anytime

Music Library - (909) 787-3137
Science Library - (909) 787-3701
Tomás Rivera Library - (909) 787-3220
Tomás Rivera Reserve Services/Cage - (909) 787-3235